VISUAL-SPATIAL learners

VISUAL-SPATIAL learners

differentiation strategies
for creating a successful classroom

ALEXANDRA SHIRES GOLON

PRUFROCK PRESS INC.
WACO, TEXAS

Library of Congress Cataloging-in-Publication Data

Golon, Alexandra Shires.
 Visual-spatial learners : differentiation strategies for creating a successful classroom /
Alexandra Shires Golon.
    p. cm.
 Includes bibliographical references.
 ISBN-13: 978-1-59363-324-0 (pbk.)
 ISBN-10: 1-59363-324-6 (pbk.)
 1. Learning, Psychology of. 2. Cognitive styles. 3. Effective teaching—United States. 4.
Learning. 5. Perception. I. Title.
 LB1060.G663 2008
 370.15'23—dc22
                        2008004737

Copyright © 2008 Prufrock Press Inc.
Edited by Jennifer Robins
Cover and Layout Design by Marjorie Parker

ISBN-13: 978-1-59363-324-0
ISBN-10: 1-59363-324-6

Printed in the United States of America.

At the time of this book's publication, all facts and figures cited are the most current
available. All telephone numbers, addresses, and Web site URLs are accurate and active.
All publications, organizations, Web sites, and other resources exist as described in the
book, and all have been verified. The authors and Prufrock Press Inc. make no warranty
or guarantee concerning the information and materials given out by organizations or
content found at Web sites, and we are not responsible for any changes that occur after
this book's publication. If you find an error, please contact Prufrock Press Inc.

Prufrock Press Inc.
P.O. Box 8813
Waco, TX 76714-8813
Phone: (800) 998-2208
Fax: (800) 240-0333
http://www.prufrock.com

Contents

chapter **1** # Learning Styles Differentiation:

Auditory-Sequential and Visual-Spatial

AS a classroom teacher, you've probably been exposed to a number of theories on learning styles and perhaps several ideas about differentiation. Some approaches can be complicated and involve lengthy assessments to fully understand each student; others require a complete revamping of the curriculum you're currently using or that your school already has approved; still others keep changing and evolving so that just when you've learned how to apply the construct, the parameters change and you're left to start all over. You won't find anything like that within these pages, however. This book provides differentiation strategies that are easy and fun to implement; it is essential for your visual-spatial learners and reinforcement for your auditory-sequential learners—the only two learning styles involved!

One definition of *differentiation* reads: "Differentiation is the adjustment of the teaching process according to the learning needs of the pupils" (Clare, 2004, ¶ 1). Another notes, "The intent of differentiating instruction is to maximize each student's growth and individual success by meeting each student where he or she is, and assisting in the learning process" (Hall, 2002, ¶ 2).

I wrote this book because I want to share just how easy differentiating for students' learning styles can be. I am a classroom teacher myself, I homeschooled for many years, and I've worked with teachers and schools in several countries. I know how challenging it is to try to meet the unique needs of each and every child. In her book, *Upside-Down Brilliance: The Visual-Spatial Learner,* Silverman (2002) wrote:

> Today's teachers must be superhuman and adapt to the children, instead of the other way around. To be a modern teacher, you must be part entertainer, part social worker, part special educator, part police officer, part ringmaster (to accommodate the range of abilities and learning styles and backgrounds and needs of all your students) and, oh yes, part enthusiast—knowledgeable of your subject matter and of the fine art of teaching. (p. 55)

When I present to teachers, I often begin by asking them to draw a rectangle, 2 inches wide by ½ inch tall—a space similar to the signature line on a personal check. Then, I ask them to place their writing instrument in their nondominant hand and sign their name within the box. I almost always hear a lot of groaning as they perform this uncomfortable task. I then ask for feedback about how it felt to sign their name this way. "Awkward," "messy," "uncomfortable," and "I can't wait to switch back" are some of the most common responses. Those who've broken their dominant hand or arm and had some experience with this task report that, although unpleasant, it wasn't as awkward as it was for their peers. Everyone reports that it wasn't their best work, nor the most efficient means of writing their name. This is what every school day feels like to a right-hemispheric, visual-spatial student sitting in a left-hemispheric, word-dominated classroom.

The concept of the visual-spatial learner, developed by Dr. Linda Silverman, director of the Gifted Development Center in Colorado (a resource center for developmentally advanced children and their parents), is based on the latest brain research and our current understanding surrounding the functions of the hemispheres. Silverman coined the term *visual-spatial learner* in 1981 to define students who think in images. In the process of testing children's intelligence, she discovered a pattern among children who scored in the highest ranges. They did so with their phenomenal abilities to solve problems presented to them visually and by excelling in the spatial tasks of intelligence tests. Analyzing hundreds of children's test results, Silverman observed two distinct learning styles: auditory-sequential and visual-spatial. Kinesthetic learners, those who learn best with hands-on activities, who often need movement to improve focus, and who learn by doing, not just watching or hearing, are included within the construct of the visual-spatial learner. The activities recommended within this book incorporate techniques that will successfully serve your kinesthetic students, as well.

Silverman's theory boils down to this: We each have two hemispheres of the brain. However, much like handedness, many of us prefer one hemisphere to the other. That preference can have dramatic implications in the classroom. It is important to note that both hemispheres work together to accomplish most cognitive tasks. It would be wrong and, in fact, silly, to conclude that a student is exclusively right- or left-brained, functioning with only half of a brain! As Hardiman (2003) noted, "Although recent research has confirmed the specialization of our brain hemispheres, we also know that the two hemispheres are continuously working in tandem to produce the rich complexities of human thought" (p. 7). In addition,

> The research data support the notion that each hemisphere has its own set of functions in information processing and thinking. However, these functions are rarely *exclusively* to only one hemisphere, and in even some simple tasks, it is possible for both hemispheres to be involved. (Sousa, 2006, p. 169)

School is geared to left-hemispheric learning. We teach in a step-by-step manner, mostly in words, and require mastery of one area before progressing to a higher level. We also tend to teach, particularly in the higher grades, in a strictly auditory fashion, leaving manipulatives and hands-on learning for younger students. Those who favor their right hemisphere are at a distinct disadvantage. Because they are presented with new material in a sequential fashion, they are required to use their weaker hemisphere (the left), rather than their stronger one.

This is analogous to someone breaking his or her arm of the dominant hand and being forced to write with the weaker hand. Eventually, and with much practice, the individual will be able to produce legible writing, but it never will be the most efficient means, nor the most beautiful writing of which he or she is capable. Only when the ability of the dominant hand is returned can this person produce his or her best work. Schools were designed for right-handed students during the ages when left-handed students were forced to write with their right hands. I still meet people in workshops all across the country who were forced to use their right hands to write even though they were not right-handed. My own grandmother, who was born completely deaf, said her biggest handicap in school wasn't that she couldn't hear, but that she was left-handed. Prejudice against our right hemisphere (which directs our left hand) continues in the emphasis on left-hemispheric educational practices. Only when we create classrooms that allow visual-spatial students to access the right hemisphere will we afford them the opportunity to produce their best work and learn in the most efficient manner for their learning style.

Understanding the specific learning style of your students and differentiating your instruction based on those learning styles may be the single most important aspect you uncover about them. To be able to teach to their strengths may be a life-changing experience for them, one that likely will leave a lasting impression for the duration of their academic career and beyond. Our personal learning style affects not only how we learn while we are students, but also how we think and approach problem solving as adults. How one thinks and learns can dramatically affect one's personal and business relationships, too.

In the 1990s, research by the Gifted Development Center staff members (Silverman, 2002) was validated using an instrument they developed called the Visual-Spatial Identifier. The results surprised even those who designed and conducted the study. The research included 750 students in grades 4–6. The children were primarily Caucasian and Hispanic, from all socioeconomic backgrounds and all IQ ranges, in an urban and rural setting.

The results demand the attention of every educator and administrator: More than one third of the study group strongly preferred a visual-spatial learning style, whereas one fourth of the group strongly preferred an auditory-sequential style. Of the group (42%) that did not lean strongly one way or the other, 30% favored a visual-spatial approach to their learning. This is an astonishing percentage of kids in the regular classroom who prefer a visual-spatial method of instruction (at least 63%) and far more than was anticipated (see Figure 1). Figure 2 shows the distribution of preferred and strongly preferred learning styles among students in the regular classroom.

In 2006, the Visual-Spatial Resource Access Team, which consisted of Linda Silverman, Linda Leviton, Steve Haas, Penny Choice, and myself, worked with the district of Page, AZ, to identify the preferred learning style of its predominantly Navajo students in grades 3–7 (DeVries & Golon, in press). The results of the study were as follows: 530 students (69%) were identified as either strongly or tending toward visual-spatial, whereas 238 students (31%) were identified as either strongly or tending toward auditory-sequential. The numbers, based on ethnicity, are as follows:

- 390, or 71%, of the Navajo students in this district were visual-spatial learners, and

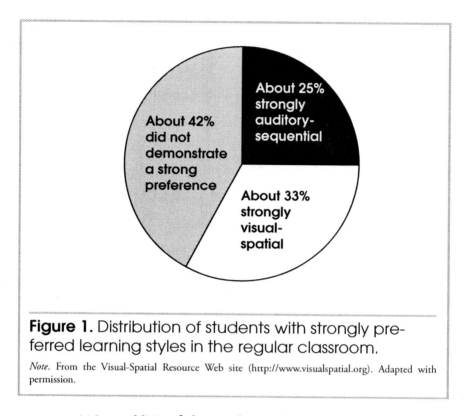

Figure 1. Distribution of students with strongly preferred learning styles in the regular classroom.

Note. From the Visual-Spatial Resource Web site (http://www.visualspatial.org). Adapted with permission.

- 118, or 66%, of the Anglo students in this district were visual-spatial learners.

Being very careful not to apply what has been discovered in the Page study to all minority groups, I want to suggest that students from culturally diverse backgrounds, particularly those who may be struggling in school, very likely may be visual-spatial learners. Anecdotally, higher visual-spatial tendencies have been observed among a number of indigenous populations throughout the U.S., Canada, and in New Zealand and Australia. Trying just a few of the techniques in this book (especially the tips for spelling or memorizing times tables) with such a student may be all that's needed to dramatically affect his or her learning experience and success level.

Further examination of the data from the Page study revealed interesting information. Within the district, students are referred to

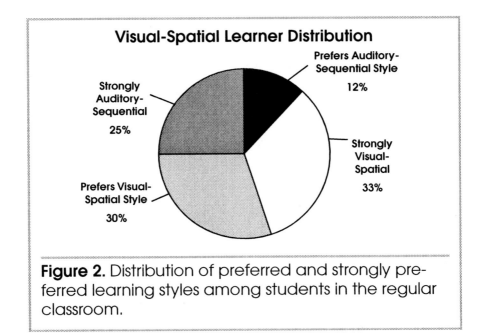

Visual-Spatial Learner Distribution

Prefers Auditory-Sequential Style 12%

Strongly Auditory-Sequential 25%

Strongly Visual-Spatial 33%

Prefers Visual-Spatial Style 30%

Figure 2. Distribution of preferred and strongly pre-ferred learning styles among students in the regular classroom.

a Student Study Team if they are not performing well academically. The team consists of parents, teachers, reading and math facilita-tors, and a school counselor. This group meets to discuss the stu-dent's areas of strengths and weaknesses and then works to devise solutions prior to testing for special education placement. After analyzing the results of the Page study, it was discovered that, on average, more than 90% of the students referred to Student Study Teams were visual-spatial learners. Additionally, of the students involved in the special education program that took part in the study, more than 90% were visual-spatial learners. The preferred learning style of the majority of the district's students, including an overwhelming number of those identified as gifted, special educa-tion, and those who had been referred for academic services, was visual-spatial. Clearly, when students' needs, particularly those dictated by their preferred learning style, were not met, many of those students found themselves requiring educational interven-tion, even remedial and/or special education services (DeVries & Golon, in press).

Anecdotally, my research, as well as the research from my former colleagues at the Gifted Development Center, has found that the number of students who favor a visual-spatial learning style increases with intellect. In classes and schools for the gifted, we have found as many as 70–75% of the students had stronger right hemispheres than left. There is evidence to suggest that some of our most revered scientists, inventors, musicians, and thinkers are, or were, strongly visual-spatial.

> The words or the language, as they are written and spoken, do not seem to play any role in my mechanism of thought. The psychical entities which seem to serve as elements in thought are certain signs and . . . images. . . . The above mentioned elements are, in my case, of visual and some of muscular type. Conventional words or other signs have to be sought for laboriously in a secondary stage. . . . (Albert Einstein, as quoted in Hadamard, 1949, pp. 142–143)

There is even more compelling research than the numbers of visual-spatial learners in a classroom to support incorporating strategies that favor the right hemisphere: Engaging the right hemisphere is good for *every* student, regardless of his or her preferred learning style. That's right! By teaching to the visual-spatial students in the room in ways that activate and engage the right hemisphere, you can more effectively reach every single student. You can begin to differentiate for students by simply addressing their right hemisphere.

Dr. Jerre Levy, a brain researcher from the University of Chicago, who is credited (along with Dr. Roger Sperry) with discovering the specific functions of each hemisphere of the brain, noted, "The right hemisphere is especially important in regulating attentional functions of both sides of the brain. Unless the right hemisphere is activated and engaged, attention is low and learning is poor" (as cited in Silverman, 2002, p. 15). Levy was referring to all students, not just those who prefer a visual-spatial learning style. In *A Whole*

New Mind: Moving From the Information Age to the Conceptual Age,
Pink (2005) wrote:

> Cognitive neuroscientists at Drexel and Northwestern universities have found that the flashes of insight that precede, "Aha!" moments are accompanied by a large burst of neural activity in the brain's right hemisphere. However, when we work out problems in a more methodical L-Directed [left-hemispheric] way, this "eureka center" remains quiet. Our ability to activate this right hemisphere capacity has become more urgent as we transition out of the Information Age. (p. 134)

So, what exactly constitutes a visual-spatial learning style versus an auditory-sequential learning style? And, how do we teach in a manner that honors visual-spatial abilities, or "activates the right hemisphere"? That's just what I hope you'll discover in this book.

Visual-spatial learners, or VSLs, are people (kids and adults) who think in images. Auditory-sequential learners, or ASLs, think in words. If you're an auditory-sequential learner, I bet you can't even imagine thinking in pictures, right? The same is true for visual learners: They can't imagine being able to think in words! A few people can think in both pictures and words, or switch between the two, but that is not as common.

Can you guess which student in the illustration on the next page is visual-spatial and which is auditory-sequential? Neither of the kids in the figure is happier than the other, nor is either one doing anything more efficiently or accurately than the other. Certainly, neither is doing anything wrong. Each child is thinking and assembling in the manner that works best for him or her. One is putting the model together in a step-by-step, follow-the-directions style, and the other is completing the project from a mental picture. There's no right or wrong way to complete the project, just as there's no right or wrong way to think and learn. There is only what works best for each of your students. Table 1 provides a quick overview of the two types of learners.

Illustrated by Buck Jones. Copyright © held by Linda K. Silverman. From Silverman, L. K. (2002). *Upside-Down Brilliance: The Visual-Spatial Learner* (p. 1). Denver, CO: DeLeon Publishing. May not be reproduced without permission. Used with permission.

In looking for a visual representation of the two hemispheres, I've not found a better illustration than Figure 3, from Linda VerLee Williams' (1983) book, *Teaching for the Two-Sided Mind: A Guide to Right Brain/Left Brain Education*. The left hemisphere is able to analyze and understand all of the parts, and the right hemisphere comprehends the whole, synthesizing the parts into one cohesive image, as illustrated with the flower in Figure 3. Again, no one is wrong in their perception, yet they are very different perspectives. Most businesses would argue that each perspective has value and should be equally rewarded, but are we preparing students to view the world from any other vantage point than the one on the left side of the figure?

I've worked with visual-spatial kids from several different countries. Many tell me that their thoughts are like movies playing in their minds. Most of the kids I've talked to say their mental pictures are in color and have so much detail, they can almost reach out and touch them. Some students tell me how they store their

Table 1

Two Types of Learners

The Auditory-Sequential Learner	The Visual-Spatial Learner
✓ Thinks mostly in words	✓ Thinks mostly in pictures
✓ Has auditory strengths	✓ Has visual strengths
✓ Is a step-by-step learner	✓ Is a whole-part learner
✓ Attends well to details	✓ Sees the big picture
✓ Follows oral directions well	✓ Reads maps well
✓ Does well at arithmetic	✓ Does well at math reasoning
✓ Learns phonics easily	✓ Learns whole words easily
✓ Can sound out spelling words	✓ Can spell words by visualizing
✓ Can write quickly and neatly	✓ Can keyboard well
✓ Can show steps of work easily	✓ Arrives at correct solutions intuitively
✓ Learns well from instructions	✓ Develops own methods of problem solving
✓ Is comfortable with one right answer	✓ Likes problems with many possible answers
✓ Is academically talented	✓ Is creatively, technologically, mechanically, emotionally or spiritually talented
✓ Can memorize math facts quickly	✓ Can tackle higher level math successfully often before mastering basic facts

Note. From *If You Could See the Way I Think: A Handbook for Visual-Spatial Kids* (p. 2), by A. S. Golon, 2005, Denver, CO: Visual-Spatial Resource. Copyright © 2005 by Alexandra Shires Golon. Reprinted with permission.

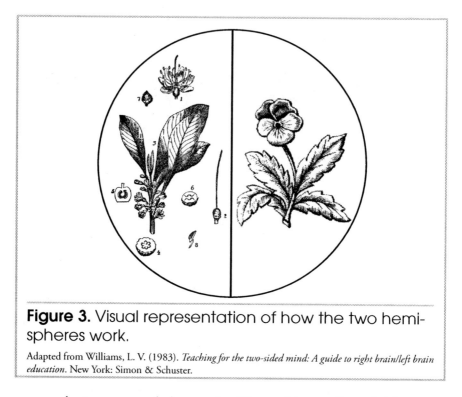

Figure 3. Visual representation of how the two hemispheres work.

Adapted from Williams, L. V. (1983). *Teaching for the two-sided mind: A guide to right brain/left brain education*. New York: Simon & Schuster.

mental pictures on shelves or in filing cabinets. One child's pictures move on a conveyer belt until he comes across the one he wants. One visual-spatial adult told me she has a chalkboard in her head that she uses to see her "To-Do" lists. I've heard from others that they use a mental whiteboard to envision spelling words and other information they want to recall. It strikes me as odd that visual-spatial students are not ever taught how to *see* what they are learning or memorizing. They've been given a gift of visualization, but don't know they have it or how to use it. Teaching them to incorporate what they are learning into a visual representation, one they draw, as one student did for me with the example he created to distinguish stalactites from stalagmites (found in caves; see Figure 4), or an image they see in their mind's eye, can mean the difference between success and failure.

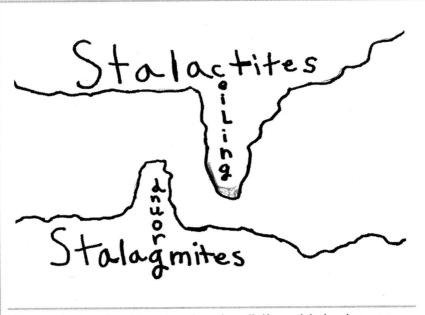

Figure 4. Student's drawing to distinguish between stalactites and stalagmites.

That's just one of many tips and techniques I'll share with you in this book. Feel free to jump around to any chapter that has the information you need right now. If you need to help your students memorize their times tables, skip right now to Chapter 9. Spelling tests have your kids frustrated? Jump to Chapter 7. Poke around and find what you need; there's no need to read this book in the order I've written it. I want this book to work for you, so use it as you see fit.

This book is full of strategies to help you instruct your visual-spatial students (and, in doing so, reinforce the learning for every student) in learning math and spelling, taking effective notes, creating written reports, using visual strategies to permanently learn new material, as well as getting and keeping your students organized in ways that are meaningful to them. Have fun discovering how your students' brains work! Then, honor your kids for the strengths they possess, no matter their preferred learning style. The auditory-sequential kids are traditionally rewarded with higher grades and an overall easier time of mastering school subjects. But, the strengths of the visual-spatial students are truly gifts, as well. Future careers will rely on the skills and talents they were born with: the ability to dream, create, invent, compose, and inspire—areas in which your VSL students were born to excel. In *A Whole New Mind*, Daniel Pink (2005) wrote that the job market has already seen significant changes—changes that only will continue as we move away from the Information Age and into the Conceptual Age, where the skills born to visual-spatial learners will be highly prized.

> We are moving from an economy and a society built on the logical, linear, computer-like capabilities of the Information Age to an economy and a society built on the inventive, empathic, big picture capabilities of what's rising in its place, the Conceptual Age. (p. 31)

Thomas West, author of *Thinking Like Einstein* (2004), agreed:

> I believe we are now at the early stages of a major transition—moving from an old world of education and work based largely on words and numbers to a new world largely based on images that are rich in content and information. (p. 16)

As educators, we can no longer ignore the importance of visual-spatial skills for current and future generations of students. We must nurture them in those students who were born with them and cultivate them in the others. We no longer can afford to teach just the basics of reading, writing, and arithmetic; today's students will face a job market completely foreign to us. West (2004) pointed out:

> For some four or five hundred years we have had our schools teaching skills that are basically those of a medieval clerk—reading, writing, counting, memorizing texts, learning for-

eign languages. . . . If we continue to turn out people who have primarily the skills . . . of the clerk, however accomplished, we may increasingly be turning out people who will . . . have less and less to sell in the global marketplace. (p. 15)

Pink (2005) also noted:

In the US, the number of graphic designers has increased tenfold in a decade; graphic designers outnumber chemical engineers by four to one. Since 1970, the United States has 30% more people earning a living as writers and 50% more earning a living by composing or performing music. . . . More Americans today work in arts, entertainment, and design than work as lawyers, accountants, and auditors. (p. 55)

So, what are we doing in today's classrooms to prepare students for this new Conceptual Age? Let's start by discovering the preferred learning style of each student.

chapter 2

Finding the Visual-Spatial Kids in Your Classroom

THERE YOU ARE!

Illustrated by Buck Jones. Copyright © held by Linda K. Silverman. From Silverman, L. K. (2002). *Upside-Down Brilliance: The Visual-Spatial Learner* (p. 317). Denver, CO: DeLeon Publishing. May not be reproduced without permission. Used with permission.

YOU probably already know who the bright auditory-sequential kids in your classroom are. They're the ones who show up for class on time, with their homework and other supplies, and are eager and ready to learn. They often earn high marks in nearly every subject, they were able to memorize their math facts with seeming ease, they spell correctly, and their homework is neatly presented with no creases or tears in the paper and includes near-perfect penmanship with no spelling, grammatical, or punctuation errors. I'm not going to offer you ways to identify or reach these kids because our traditional left-hemispheric, step-by-step approach works just fine for this type of learner. But, I do want you to have a clear picture of how to distinguish between the auditory-sequential learners and the visual-spatial learners in your room. Keep in mind, there is not a defined distinction between the two, rather a continuum on which many children fall strongly toward one end or the other. There is a significant percentage of the student body that prefers their right hemisphere to their left. It's for these kids that this book was written.

Visual-Spatial Learners

Below are some descriptions that may help you discover which of your kids are visual-spatial.

The Pilers

These are the kids who pile all of their belongings, some horizontally, some vertically. They seldom "file" anything. In fact, to insist that they file and organize the way an auditory-sequential learner might do would cause them to never be able to find another homework assignment again! And, *never* help the colleague who is a piler by organizing for him or her—even if you do have to share office space!

SEQUENTIAL   SPATIAL

The Fidgeters

Visual-spatial kids typically are also kinesthetic learners, meaning they take in information through their senses. It can be quite challenging for them to sit still, and this can cause them to have difficulty focusing on learning, so I suggest you let them move! This may sound counterintuitive; traditionally, children are expected to be seated properly and at attention in order to learn. However, proper posture and attention often are at the expense of the visual-spatial child's ability to focus and retain information. In Chapter 12, we'll talk about strategies that keep your classroom from becoming too chaotic, yet honor the kinesthetic needs of some of your students.

Illustrated by Buck Jones. Copyright © held by Linda K. Silverman. From Silverman, L. K. (2002). *Upside-Down Brilliance: The Visual-Spatial Learner* (p. 218). Denver, CO: DeLeon Publishing. May not be reproduced without permission. Used with permission.

The Tinkerers

These are the kids who love to take things apart to see how they work—while you hold your breath that they'll put it all back together again! For many, there is no intimidation about a computer or other equipment—they just seem to understand how to manipulate it, take it apart, or otherwise use it to their advantage. This cartoon is actually a drawing representing my husband who, at 7 years old, rescued the family vacuum cleaner from the curbside trash pile, took it apart, cleaned it, oiled it, and gave his mom a bill!

Illustrated by Buck Jones. Copyright © held by Alexandra Shires Golon. From Golon, A. S. (2002). *If You Could See the Way I Think: A Handbook for Visual-Spatial Kids* (p. 16). Denver, CO: DeLeon Publishing. May not be reproduced without permission. Used with permission.

The Daydreamers

You know those kids who choose a seat at the back of the class, next to the window? Then, while you're in the middle of the most important lecture, you find them staring out into space, not paying attention to a word? Well, guess what? If they're visual-spatial learners, they're actually hanging on your every word, busily creating pictures in their minds to go with what they are hearing. To ask them to turn their heads toward you would be to completely interrupt their learning. Because visual-spatial kids think in pictures, they must translate your words into the permanent mental images they will use later to recall that new information. For many, the only way to do that is to be focusing, visually, on something else so that auditorally, they can devote 100% of their attention on you.

Distractibility and daydreaming during reading class may be . . . early indicators of creativity and innovative thinking, "symptoms" that will bolster her career as a scriptwriter or music video producer. A student's trouble understanding language may cause him to do much less of his thinking with words, as a result of which he strengthens his visual and spatial thinking, destined to serve him well two decades later in his career as a mechanical engineer . . . (Levine, 2002, p. 37)

So, how do you distinguish the visual-spatial students from the true daydreamers? Gently bring them into the conversation by asking what they've heard so far. Give them time to translate their images into words. Do their mental pictures match what you've been presenting? I'll bet your students will surprise you with just how well they really are listening. There are more tips to keep your visual-spatial students' attention during auditory lectures in Chapter 12.

The Imaginative Kids

Visual-spatial learners have very vivid imaginations, which lend to wonderful creative inventions, storytelling, and so on. These are the kids whose imaginations will allow for the inventions and advanced technology that will one day take us to Mars or allow us to live on the moon! As one parent noted,

> I think most VS girls play with dolls longer and more intensely than their non-VS counterparts do. E is 9 and most girls her age are not playing with dolls much; in fact, its hard for her to find a friend who will play dolls with her. The girls who do [play dolls] seem to have VS traits. E creates all sorts of things for her dolls—she makes food out of clay for them, last night she made friendship necklaces for them. (K.C.)

The "I Don't Know How I Know, I Just Know" Kids

Visual-spatial learners are quite intuitive. This is especially true in math. Because they see the big picture, they often, and quite mysteriously, come up with correct answers to problems, yet they absolutely are unable to show any steps to their work—there just aren't any steps to show! The most important message you can give them, as their teacher, is that you respect their way of thinking and that you don't, in any way, question how they got their answer. When there is mutual respect for how each other thinks, the student often can be asked to support his or her mental methods with more traditionally accepted, demonstrated work. In Chapter 9, you'll find ways to honor visual-spatial kids for their intuition and unique methods for obtaining answers, yet teach them to "show their work," so they can always get full credit for right answers.

Illustrated by Buck Jones. Copyright © held by Linda K. Silverman. From Silverman, L. K. (2002). *Upside-Down Brilliance: The Visual-Spatial Learner* (p. 93). Denver, CO: DeLeon Publishing. May not be reproduced without permission. Used with permission.

The Time Phobics

Most VSLs can't quickly translate their pictures into words (or numbers, if it's a math test) when they are under pressure or know they have a limited amount of time. I'll discuss some strategies for helping your students with timed tests in Chapter 13, "The Dreaded Timed Test." In the meantime, get rid of those timed tests altogether! Timed tests were invented in the early part of the last century to create efficient factory workers who could repeat mundane tasks in quick order. Your students are not going to grow up and seek such jobs—those jobs have been replaced with robots and computer-guided equipment. It's time we stop preparing students for jobs of yesteryear by insisting they perfect skills that just aren't necessary for jobs in the 21st century.

The "I'll Be There in Just a Minute" Kids

Yeah, right! It appears to be a universal truth that visual-spatial kids and adults have absolutely no concept of the passage of time. So, "one minute" rarely equates to anything close to 60 seconds! So absorbed in creative play or the project of the moment, these students often resist transitioning from one subject to the next. And, with that noted lack of time comes no sense of how to plan for long-term assignments, either. We'll talk about helping your students understand the passage of time including how to plan for long-term assignments in Chapter 11, "Organizational Skills."

The Humorous Creative Types

Humor resides in the right hemisphere of the brain. Most visual-spatial kids use it liberally. They come up with the funniest jokes, the greatest plays on words, and they're the first ones laughing at your puns.

LADIES AND GENTLEMEN, I DON'T HAVE MY HOMEWORK DONE... AND LET ME TELL YOU WHY!!!

MISS JONES

Illustrated by Buck Jones. Copyright © held by Linda K. Silverman. From Silverman, L. K. (2002). *Upside-Down Brilliance: The Visual-Spatial Learner* (p. 272). Denver, CO: DeLeon Publishing. May not be reproduced without permission. Used with permission.

You may find that some of your students fit more than one—or even all—of these categories. They're just a little closer to one end of the continuum than your other students and they're the ones who really need these differentiation strategies!

The VSL Quiz for Kids

Here are some traits, in the form of a questionnaire, that are typical of visual-spatial learners. The first quiz presented is the VSL Quiz for Kids from the handbook, *If You Could See the Way I Think: A Handbook for Visual-Spatial Kids* (Golon, 2005). You're welcome to photocopy it and let your students complete it, if you'd like. The second quiz is one you can complete about each of your students. Please note that not every characteristic will fit every student. We each have two hemispheres, and we require the use of both for nearly everything we do. As I mentioned earlier, the extent to which a student is auditory-sequential or visual-spatial lies somewhere on a continuum; some students are extremely visual-spatial, whereas others are only slightly so. But, just as most of us are strongly right- or left-handed, most of us are strongly right- or left-hemispheric. You'll find more anecdotes and information about each of the questions following the quiz. It has been my experience that if a child answers "Yes" to nine or more questions, he or she is very likely a visual-spatial learner.

A student need not answer "yes" to all of the questions on the quiz to be a VSL. You might find the following explanations and scenarios to each of the questions interesting. If your students had trouble answering any of the questions, read the appropriate parts within this chapter and see if the questions become easier or clearer for them. There will be varying degrees of visual-spatial abilities among the kids in your class. But, remember, creating a visual-spatial classroom will help every child, not just the visual-spatial students.

1. *Do you think mainly in pictures?* If your students are not sure whether they are thinking in pictures or words, try this trick: Ask them to spell their name backwards, spell your name, or answer a simple question. As they answer, watch to see whether they look to their upper left or upper right while answering the question. Tell them not to look at you, but to "find" their answer, somewhere in space. A look to the upper left to "see" the answer means they are accessing the right hemisphere of the brain, where images are stored. A look to the upper right means they are using their left hemisphere, or using words not images. If they look straight up, they could be relying on both hemispheres. If they rely on the left hemisphere more (meaning they looked to the upper right when searching for the answer), they are likely auditory-sequential learners. If they use the right hemisphere more (meaning they looked to the upper left when searching for the answer), they are likely visual-spatial learners. If they closed their eyes, go on to the next question! (Only a few of the kids I've worked with looked down, but I was still able to determine whether they had looked first to their left or right.)

Name: _____ Date: _____

Are You a Visual-Spatial Learner?

		Yes	No
1.	Do you think mainly in pictures?	☐	☐
2.	Are you good at solving puzzles or mazes?	☐	☐
3.	Do you like to build with LEGO™, K'Nex™, blocks, etc.?	☐	☐
4.	Do you often lose track of time?	☐	☐
5.	Do you know things without being able to tell how or why?	☐	☐
6.	Do you remember how to get to places you have visited only once?	☐	☐
7.	Can you feel what others are feeling?	☐	☐
8.	Do you remember what you see and forget what you hear?	☐	☐
9.	Do you solve problems in unusual ways?	☐	☐
10.	Do you have a wild imagination?	☐	☐
11.	Do you love music, dance, art, or drama?	☐	☐
12.	Can you see things in your mind's eye from different perspectives?	☐	☐
13.	Do others think you are unorganized?	☐	☐
14.	Do you love playing on the computer?	☐	☐
15.	Do you have trouble spelling words correctly?	☐	☐
16.	Do you like taking things apart to see how they work?	☐	☐

If you answered **yes** to at least **nine** of the above questions, you are most likely a visual-spatial learner.

Note. From *If You Could See the Way I Think: A Handbook for Visual-Spatial Kids* (p. 6), by A. S. Golon, 2005, Denver, CO: Visual-Spatial Resource. Copyright © 2005 by Alexandra Shires Golon. Reprinted with permission.

Name: _____ Date: _____

Is the Student
a Visual-Spatial Learner?

	Yes	No
1. Does the student think mainly in pictures?	❑	❑
2. Is he or she good at solving puzzles or mazes?	❑	❑
3. Does he or she like to build with LEGO™, K'Nex™, blocks, etc.?	❑	❑
4. Does he or she often lose track of time?	❑	❑
5. Does he or she know things without being able to tell how or why?	❑	❑
6. Does he or she remember how to get to places visited only once?	❑	❑
7. Can he or she feel what others are feeling?	❑	❑
8. Does he or she remember what is seen and forget what is heard?	❑	❑
9. Does he or she solve problems in unusual ways?	❑	❑
10. Does he or she have a wild imagination?	❑	❑
11. Does he or she love music, dance, art, or drama?	❑	❑
12. Can he or she see things in the mind's eye from different perspectives?	❑	❑
13. Do others think he or she is unorganized?	❑	❑
14. Does he or she love playing on the computer?	❑	❑
15. Does he or she have trouble spelling words correctly?	❑	❑
16. Does he or she like taking things apart to see how they work?	❑	❑

If you answered **yes** to at least **nine** of the above questions, this student is most likely a visual-spatial learner.

Note. From *The Visual-Spatial Classroom: Differentiation Strategies That Engage Every Learner* (p. 19), by A. S. Golon, 2006, Denver, CO: Visual-Spatial Resource. Copyright © 2006 by Alexandra Shires Golon. Reprinted with permission.

2. Are you good at solving puzzles or mazes? Lots of VSL kids I know are amazing at solving all kinds of puzzles: jigsaw, three-dimensional, and others. I've heard stories of very young children turning the pieces to a jigsaw puzzle over so they could assemble them by the shape only, with the back side facing up! Other parents have noted that their children mix all of the pieces of several puzzles together in order to make them more challenging. These kids easily can find their way through mazes (this is the child you want with you on the next field trip because he'll remember where you parked!), three-dimensional puzzles, and games like Tetris™, Rush Hour™, Shape by Shape™, and Tangrams.

3. Do you like to build with LEGO™, K'Nex™, blocks, etc.? What type of learner do you think creates those spectacular LEGO™ sets? Definitely a visual-spatial learner! The directions don't come with words, only pictures, so you need to be able to manipulate objects in your mind's eye in order to create all the amazing figures they come up with using a mix of squares and rectangles. The same is true with K'Nex™, Zome™, and other construction toys.

However, these kids don't need formal toys for creating—recycled towel rolls and some Scotch tape work just as well. I hear stories from parents who have to ration the amount of tape their children are allowed each week because they are constantly building and creating with toilet paper rolls, empty tissue boxes, and whatever else they can get their hands on. I also hear from teachers who've learned to ask for such recyclables to be brought in for their art and science centers, saving them precious budget money on art supplies.

Illustrated by Buck Jones. Copyright © held by Linda K. Silverman. From Silverman, L. K. (2002). *Upside-Down Brilliance: The Visual-Spatial Learner* (p. 8). Denver, CO: DeLeon Publishing. May not be reproduced without permission. Used with permission.

4. Do you often lose track of time? These are the "I'll be there in just a minute" kids mentioned previously. They're the ones who offer this response, but then several minutes will pass and they haven't moved. Then they're scratching their head wondering why you're so upset when you only asked them to come a couple of seconds ago. I've mentioned before that most VSLs (kids and adults) don't have a very good idea about how time flies when they're having fun. Understanding how time passes may not be their strength, but understanding space is. When they're in a building, they are very aware of what room is directly above or below them. They can easily find the staircase or elevator in an unfamiliar building. Strategies for helping teach time management are provided in Chapter 11.

5. Do you know things without being able to tell how or why? The kids that answer "yes" to this feel almost as though they have extrasensory perception or really great intuition. They just know how certain things work (like computers) or how to take something apart and fix it, even if they never have before. Most VSLs have pictures in their minds and they don't even know how those pictures got there. The best part is, the pictures are almost always right. And, because they're images, they are permanent and easily can be recalled.

6. Do you remember how to get to places you have visited only once?

A. has always had an amazing sense of direction. When as a toddler he would say from his pram I was going the wrong way, initially you would ignore "the silly baby"—it didn't take long to work out the amount of times "the silly baby" was actually right! I learned to listen so by

" MOMMY, YOU MISSED YOUR TURN."

Illustrated by Buck Jones. Copyright © held by Linda K. Silverman. From Silverman, L. K. (2002). *Upside-Down Brilliance: The Visual-Spatial Learner* (p. 125). Denver, CO: DeLeon Publishing. May not be reproduced without permission. Used with permission.

age 5 I would trust him find my car again in those giant supermarket car parks because invariably I would get lost. (J.M., parent)

I've received several e-mails about children who seem to be prewired with Global Positioning Systems (GPS) in their brains. Whether it's from their stroller or the backseat, they pipe up with the correct direction, and they're usually right. Visual-spatial learners often find themselves wondering why others can't picture exactly how to get somewhere when the route seems obvious to

Illustrated by Buck Jones. Copyright © held by Linda K. Silverman. From Silverman, L. K. (2002). *Upside-Down Brilliance: The Visual-Spatial Learner* (p. 84). Denver, CO: DeLeon Publishing. May not be reproduced without permission. Used with permission.

them. They're unable to listen to a series of directions auditorally (e.g., how to get somewhere, how to complete an assignment) and remember all of it unless they've been able to create a mental picture or see a map.

7. Can you feel what others are feeling? These are the kids, even young preschoolers, who can walk into a room and immediately sense if their teacher or a fellow student is having a bad day. Lots of

VSLs tell me that they just sense when someone needs a good hug. Many feel empathy toward animals, even insects, and have difficulty visiting zoos or other places where animals are enclosed. They will rescue a spider and take it outside rather than let someone swat it. The ability to read another person's emotions and respond appropriately will help these children throughout their lives.

8. *Do you remember what you see and forget what you hear?* When listening to auditory lectures, visual-spatial kids are more likely to remember what was taught if there were overheads, maps, or pictures used as well. Better yet is the use of hands-on activities such as experiments, creating timelines, making mobiles of important facts, incorporating metaphors to relate learning to something your students already understand, using music to memorize new material, employing fantasy as a means of experiential learning, and providing direct experience opportunities (e.g., field trips, experiments, hands-on activities) whenever you can. Because visual-spatial learners remember what they see and not necessarily what they hear, be sure your students are seeing and doing, not just hearing or reading. This book is full of these types of strategies, and *all* of your students will benefit from these techniques.

Illustrated by Buck Jones. Copyright © held by Alexandra Shires Golon. From Golon, A. S. (2002). *If You Could See the Way I Think: A Handbook for Visual-Spatial Kids* (p. 11). Denver, CO: DeLeon Publishing. May not be reproduced without permission. Used with permission.

As Mel Levine (2002) observed in one of his patients,

One girl's parents commented to me perceptively, "She remembers things she's seen so much better than things she's heard. She is terrifically observant. She remembers what you're wearing and the expression on your face. She helps me find the car when we park in the garage at the mall. But then she instantly forgets a telephone message." . . . Kids need to make maximum use of their strongest pathway of input whenever possible. A child whose visual-spatial input is well received should try to do a lot of that kind of imaging . . . (p. 97)

9. *Do you solve problems in unusual ways?* Visual-spatial learners naturally think outside the box, finding solutions that others rarely think of. They don't need anyone to teach them how to think that way. I once met a 10-year-old visual-spatial girl who had begged her mom to save a large box. She said, "I need the box so I can think outside the box!" The ability to naturally think of creative and unusual ideas is a great talent, but many students have to wait until college or a career to appreciate what a gift that is. Encourage your students to explore different routes to a solution, and then narrow their methods to the most efficient solution. By teaching them to be open-minded in discovering ways to problem solve, you'll be tapping into their creative right hemispheres.

Illustrated by Buck Jones. Copyright © held by Linda K. Silverman. From Silverman, L. K. (2002). *Upside-Down Brilliance: The Visual-Spatial Learner* (Front Cover). Denver, CO: DeLeon Publishing. May not be reproduced without permission. Used with permission.

10. *Do you have a wild imagination?* VSLs usually tell fantastic stories and they often enjoy role-playing games. Some can create mental images so real that they can feel, touch, or even smell what they are imagining. It is their wonderful imagination that allows them to take common household items and turn them into new and fun inventions.

Many VSLs find joy and excitement in everything they do—even if it's something as simple as watching bugs make their way through the grass. But, they become bored and tune out when listening to lectures. Some may call this daydreaming; others might think they have an attention issue. This book was written to help you guide your visual-spatial students toward using the stronger hemisphere of their brains, the right hemisphere, in everything they do. This is accomplished by incorporating humor, color, music, metaphors, and other visual aids in your classroom. I'll offer some specific tips for helping students stay focused in Chapter 12.

11. *Do you love music, dance, art, or drama?* Visual-spatial learners often are talented artists. Some find they love to paint or build, or that they love to listen to music, to play a musical instrument, to sing, or to dance. Others enjoy pretending they are characters from books and movies. Still others express an appreciation for the arts. For most, paintings seem to call out to them and music truly moves them. They are typically art appreciators at an early age. You can help kindle this passion for the arts by including more of it in your lessons. A study of any period in history can readily include the art—even if it's cave paintings—of the era. The same is true with music. As a teacher, I incorporated large, visual timelines into history lessons that included the scientific breakthroughs, music, and art of the period we were studying. Students remember historical facts better when they relate those facts to other information. Understanding the music, art, or science that was going on during the reign of a particular monarch or term of a specific president can provide insight and offer connections for students.

12. *Can you see things in your mind's eye from different perspectives?* When the student is looking at a picture of a building, can he imagine what the opposite side looks like? When she is in a two-story building, can she tell what room is directly above or below the room she is in? For example,

> [E. is] also good at designing spaces. When my daughter was little she spent hours creating apartments, coffee shops, and town houses for her Barbie dolls. What was different about her Barbie villages was their three-dimensional quality. If you stood on a stool and looked down, the apartment was laid out like a floor plan, if that makes any sense. (K.C., parent)

The ability to turn things around or upside down in one's mind can sometimes cause problems with reading and writing. The letters can roll and flip, mentally, so that one letter becomes another. Some visual-spatial learners have trouble because the letters *p*, *b*, *d*, and *q* are the exact same shape: a ball and a stick! For those who have trouble handwriting because the letters turn and twist in their mind's eye, I highly recommend keyboard instruction (this is addressed in more detail in Chapter 6). On a keyboard, those same letters are *P*, *B*, *D*, and *Q*, so students don't mix them up. When students use keyboards, they're using both of their hands to type, which means both hemispheres of their brains are at work. Anything that keeps both hemispheres active helps them succeed!

13. *Do others think you are unorganized?* Do your visual-spatial students keep their work area looking like this boy's filing cabinet? Are they able to find what they need when they need it? Lots of people think that the person on the right needs help getting organized. But, if he can find just what he needs when he needs it, then his organization system works just fine for him. However, if your students can't locate their homework assignments, or they're losing other important things, then they do need some help with

organization. We'll talk about specific organization strategies in Chapter 11.

14. *Do you love playing on the computer?* Almost all VSLs have a love affair with their computers. They can manipulate the computer in ways that others just can't figure out. (They're the kids you want helping you install new software or set up e-mail accounts!) When a person has a strong right hemisphere, which VSLs do, he or she intuitively understands, or can quickly learn, how to operate computers. One middle school teacher has his students do everything on the computer. Even parents are notified of assignments via

Illustrated by Buck Jones. Copyright © held by Alexandra Shires Golon. From Golon, A.S. (2004). *Raising Topsy-Turvy Kids: Successfully Parenting Your Visual-Spatial Child* (p. 23). Denver, CO: DeLeon Publishing. May not be reproduced without permission. Used with permission.

daily e-mail announcements. It's pretty difficult to lose your paper (or claim the dog ate it!) when it's on your laptop.

15. *Do you have trouble spelling words correctly?* Spelling has been taught for generations in a sequential manner with odd rules. Who can possibly remember when "i" comes before "e"—especially if the rule is broken so many times? One student had to repeat the word "species" on his spelling list week after week because he dutifully remembered that rule and consistently misspelled it "speceis." Our written language makes little or no sense, particularly to one who thinks in images, not words. In Chapter 7, I'll show you ways

to help teach spelling words as images so that your visual-spatial students can start acing their spelling tests.

16. *Do you like taking things apart to see how they work?* Most VSLs have an insatiable curiosity to understand how everything works—from telephones to toasters to computers! Whenever something stops working in my house, I wait until everyone has had a chance to tinker with it before I replace it. These kids are builders and inventors, too. A supply of recyclable materials and some Scotch tape often are all you need in an invention center or discovery zone. Here's what one mother of a visual-spatial girl wrote:

> . . . I think her VS traits show up in ways that don't fit the general description. She loves to design and take things apart but not mechanical stuff. She takes apart her lip gloss and wants to understand the components in makeup, which requires studying chemistry. (K.C.)

The Results

Now, have your students add up all the questions they answered "yes" and "no" to. If they answered "yes" to nine or more questions, they probably are visual-spatial learners. Take a look at how many VSLs you have in your class. I've included a chart for you to log your students on page 38. Are you surprised at the kids who prefer this learning style? Are you surprised by how strongly some are visual-spatial? I once administered this quiz to a class at a private school for gifted children and the teacher was quite stunned—a full 80% of his class was strongly visual-spatial.

Now, consider grouping your students by learning style for specific tasks or subjects. For example, you could group together the strongly and moderately visual-spatial students to work on discovering methods of simple division while you teach the auditory-sequential students the traditional, step-by-step manner. Or, you could combine students into teams of auditory-sequential learners and visual-spatial learners to do group reports. The auditory-sequential students could be responsible for the written aspect of the report, while the visual-spatial students could produce the corresponding maps, dioramas, or costumes. There are a number of ways you can group students together based on their learning styles that will help engage every learner and allow him or her to succeed. The added bonus is that students will be exposed to the type of cooperative learning and team building necessary in their future careers. Few successful adults achieve great levels entirely on their own. Most rely on aides, editors, secretaries, and other types of assistants who play a vital role in the team's success.

Where Do We Go From Here?

Since the creation of modern school, teachers and curricula have been teaching to the left hemisphere, in step-by-step directions with material that builds on previous learning. This is an approach that leaves visual-spatial learners out in the cold. For VSLs, the left hemisphere never can become as efficient or successful as the right hemisphere. The right is just simply stronger for them. The comparison of a right-handed person breaking the right arm is worth repeating. Certainly, right-handers can learn to write legibly with their left hand, but it never will be as comfortable or efficient, nor will the writing ever be as legible as what they are capable of producing with their right hand. This is what we've done to right-hemispheric thinkers for centuries. It's time to stop

VSL Quiz for Kids Results

Use this log to record those students who appear strongly, moderately, or mildly visual-spatial versus those students who appear strongly, moderately, or mildly auditory-sequential. This will make grouping students who learn similarly easier.

Strongly Visual-Spatial Students (14–16 "Yes" responses; 0–2 "No" responses)

_____ _____ _____

_____ _____ _____

_____ _____ _____

Moderately Visual-Spatial Students (11–13 "Yes" responses; 3–5 "No" responses)

_____ _____ _____

_____ _____ _____

_____ _____ _____

Mildly Visual-Spatial Students (9–10 "Yes" responses; 6–7 "No" responses)

_____ _____ _____

_____ _____ _____

_____ _____ _____

Strongly Auditory-Sequential Students (14–16 "No" responses; 0–2 "Yes" responses)

_____   _____   _____

_____   _____   _____

_____   _____   _____

Moderately Auditory-Sequential Students (11–13 "No" responses; 3–5 "Yes" responses)

_____   _____   _____

_____   _____   _____

_____   _____   _____

Mildly Auditory-Sequential Students (9–10 "No" responses; 6–7 "Yes" responses)

_____   _____   _____

_____   _____   _____

_____   _____   _____

Note. From _The Visual-Spatial Classroom: Differentiation Strategies That Engage Every Learner_ (p. 31), by A. S. Golon, 2006, Denver, CO: Visual-Spatial Resource. Copyright © 2006 by Alexandra Shires Golon. Reprinted with permission.

insisting that those with stronger right hemispheres rely solely on their left for learning and retaining new material.

For many VSLs, the traditional classroom presents a real challenge. Schools were designed for auditory-sequential learners. Auditory-sequential learners remember what they hear; we teach by talking. They love learning new material that builds on what they've already mastered; we teach following the same approach. School is a perfect fit for the auditory-sequential learner. But, there's no reason it also can't be a perfect fit for the visual-spatial learner.

> Learning does not occur in classrooms; it occurs in students' minds. The role of the teacher and the classroom he creates is to offer possibilities in such a way that students will both want and be able to learn. The richer the banquet we lay, the more students will partake and the longer they will stay at the table. (Williams, 1983, p. 194)

You probably can think of at least one visual-spatial student who is falling through the cracks academically. You have the opportunity to save that student. Armed with an understanding of how the brain of a visual-spatial learner is wired, combined with a willingness to honor that learning style, these children no longer have to feel inferior to their auditory-sequential classmates.

In *A Mind at a Time*, Mel Levine (2002) wrote:

> It's taken for granted in adult society that we cannot all be ...skilled in every area of learning and mastery. Nevertheless, we apply tremendous pressure on our children to be good at *everything*. Every day they are expected to shine in math, reading, writing, speaking, spelling, memorization, comprehension, problem solving, socialization, athletics, and following verbal directions. (p. 23)

It is critical that, as teachers, we honor these students for their strengths and not penalize them for the way in which their brains are wired. The 21st century is an amazing time to be a visual-spatial learner. The gifts these children were born with will allow them to become great surgeons, design beautiful buildings, compose moving music, create exciting computer games, design computer-animated movies, or become a musician, artist, or dancer. School is an important pathway for reaching those goals. Surgeons, architects, engineers, designers, composers, and artists go through many years of school so that they can qualify for these jobs. Visual-spatial learners, teamed with compassionate teachers to guide them, can make school work to their advantage.

chapter 3

Are Boys More Visual-Spatial Than Girls?

Why Gender Matters in Every Classroom

NEARLY every time I present, whether it's to an audience of parents or teachers, about 15 minutes into my discussion (following some typical characteristics of visual-spatial learners), I am asked, "Are boys more visual-spatial than girls?" or "Are there more visual-spatial boys than girls?" I tend not to answer right away, waiting instead until we've discussed more about identifying traits of children who favor this learning style. Eventually, I ask participants to write down the name of a child (their own or a student) that they are fairly certain fits the profile of a visual-spatial learner. With a show of hands I ask, "Who among you wrote down the name of a boy?" and "Who among you wrote down the name of a girl?" Almost without fail, boys are pegged by the majority of the participants and only a few have chosen a female student. Why is that? Why do teachers and parents seek out advice on behalf of their male students and children significantly more often than for their female students and children?

When I first began studying this learning style in earnest, I was concerned that I was looking through a very biased lens. Both of my children are visual-spatial and male, my husband is visual-spatial and male, 80% or more of my students were visual-spatial and male, and more than 90% of the families that had hired me to consult with or advocate on their behalf asked me to do so on behalf of their male visual-spatial children. Even the cartoonist who created all the renderings of my life with my children and students was male and (you guessed it) visual-spatial. He inadvertently drew every visual-spatial child as a male and every auditory-sequential (left-hemispheric) child as female. At one point, I had to ask that a rendering of my son manipulating a computer while still in diapers be drawn as a young girl because we had so few cartoons depicting female visual-spatial learners. (They do exist, in case you're still wondering.) And so, I began a quest of my own to read as much as I could find regarding the differences between the sexes when it comes to spatial abilities, particularly as related to successful classroom learning.

Historically, boys and men have long excelled in spatial ability tests compared to girls and women. Some have proposed a hunter-gatherer theory, predicting that men excel in spatial abilities such as navigation, map reading, and mental rotations because survival depended on the ability to hunt, hurl a spear through space at a moving target, and find one's way home. Women, on the other hand, required better spatial location memory in their work as gatherers and keeping a watchful eye over home and hearth (Silverman & Eals, 1992). Long the nurturing gender, women required skills of empathy to care for their young and nurse others. Other theories have postulated that spatial abilities are further enhanced by experience and that, once endowed with ability in a particular area, the individual continues to select activities that serve to further increase ability in that domain. We see this in the selection of many extracurricular activities where those with an innate ability to draw, for example, often choose visual arts classes. This certainly has been the case with children I've worked with and who enjoy building with LEGOs, for example—most follow that passion and transfer their architectural skills to other building and construction toys.

So, are boys more visual-spatial than girls? Well, it could be successfully argued that they appear to be more visual-spatial at a younger age than girls:

> . . . some of the regions involved in mechanical reasoning, visual targeting and spatial reasoning appeared to mature four to eight years earlier in boys. The parts that handle verbal fluency, handwriting and recognizing familiar faces matured several years earlier in girls. (Ripley, 2005, p. 55)

We have ample research to demonstrate that young boys don't appear as "school ready" (read "left hemispheric"), or able to manage pencil-and-paper tasks, as early as girls do. Michael Gurian (2001) of The Gurian Institute wrote that there are stronger connecting pathways within the female cerebellum brain than the male, providing more superior language and fine-motor skills for girls than for boys. A more active frontal lobe, which facilitates speech, thought, and emotion, allows for improved verbal communication in girls (Gurian, 2001, p. 20)—all of which help girls appear more ready for school and school-based learning than their male counterparts.

Researchers at Virginia Tech "found that . . . the areas of the brain involved in language and fine motor skills mature about six years earlier in girls than in boys" (Sax, 2005, p. 93). "For a 1,500 Hz tone . . . the average girl baby had an acoustic brain response about 80 percent greater than the response of the average baby boy . . . that range of sound is critical for understanding speech" (Sax, 2005, p. 17). This is particularly important when thinking about speech from a female voice (and note that most elementary school teachers are female). Sax went on to write that, "the female-male difference in hearing only gets bigger as kids get older" (p. 17). This is not an area in which teachers can expect boys to catch up; they are biologically wired against accurately hearing instructions, lectures, and other important classroom information. Male students seated at the back of the room, or farthest from where you normally speak, cannot hope to hear what you are saying. One option is to fix the classroom arrangement. If rearranging desks into a horseshoe or other format that allows for equal opportunity to hear is not an option, you may want to consider moving the boys up front.

The problem may lie, however, in what we regard as "school ready" skills. Seldom do we assess or monitor the development of spatial abilities, often an area of strength for many boys. Geography, an area in which most visual-spatial learners excel, is not typically introduced until the later grades, nor is higher level mathematics. Instead, early math often is the rote memorization of seemingly meaningless facts and figures, which manages to turn off many of our nation's natural-born mathematicians.

Here's something to consider: Boys represent 90% of the discipline problems, 80% of the dropouts, and 66% of the identified learning disabled in America's classrooms (Gurian, 2001, p. 56). No wonder the teachers and parents of boys far outnumber the teachers and parents of girls who request my services.

Certainly there are plenty of visual-spatial women. Many visual-spatial girls have grown up to pursue careers as mathematicians, pilots, artists, musicians, designers, architects, and other "right-hemispheric" pursuits. So, why the disparity in what classroom teachers see, particularly during the elementary school years? My personal observation is that girls, while they may have strong visual-spatial abilities and show a preference for the right hemisphere of the brain (as demonstrated by their responses to incorporating music, rhythm, and other instructional strategies that speak to that hemisphere), are predisposed to please their teacher and are not inclined to act out if bored, unchallenged, or disengaged. Most girls would never dream of complaining that they did not understand, or "see," the material being covered—they would simply find a way to compensate or appear not to be able to do the work at all. Boys, on the other hand, tend to not have any qualms about verbalizing their displeasure with a situation, acting out on a classmate if they are bored, and otherwise becoming a behavior issue in the classroom. And so, boys are referred to education specialists, psychologists, and counselors for education-related and/or behavior issues, whereas girls typically are not.

I have long been plagued with the question: Is this a "boy" problem or a teaching problem? Take no offense educators, I am a classroom teacher myself, but my work with practitioners in classrooms all over the world has convinced me that there is a significant population of male students for whom the problem is one of instruction. Although well intentioned, too many of the teachers I have worked with continue to deliver instruction in an old and tired format of word-based lecture and textbooks. Their classrooms might be havens for word thinkers who can easily remember facts and figures and recite them on demand, but there is a significant population many educators have let fall through the cracks: gifted children, students with learning disabilities (gifted and otherwise), English Language Learners, minority children, students who excel in the arts, and a whole host of other visual-spatial learners for whom the written and spoken word is the least effective instructional method. Many of these are boys, but there are girls in that mix, as well.

This book is filled with a number of strategies teachers can employ to help visual-spatial learners (both boys and girls) succeed in school. I hope you'll try at least a few of the techniques and rescue a gifted visual-spatial learner from the fate that has befallen so many before. And, because I believe so strongly in the value of spatial abilities and their application to successful careers in the 21st century, I would encourage students who don't necessarily identify with a visual-spatial learning style to participate and become more proficient in activities of spatial awareness by reading maps, communicating directions, playing and building with construction toys, manipulating puzzles and mazes, and the like.

chapter **4** **Reading**

Illustrated by Buck Jones. Copyright © held by Linda K. Silverman. From Silverman, L. K. (2002). *Upside-Down Brilliance: The Visual-Spatial Learner* (p. 88). Denver, CO: DeLeon Publishing. May not be reproduced without permission. Used with permission.

BEING taught to read often is a visual-spatial learner's first exposure to true left-hemispheric instruction. Most schools and teachers use a phonetic approach to reading. However, many visual-spatials learn to read using a whole word, or sight word, method. VSLs have a hard time with phonics because it breaks down words into the smallest sounds, such as: ra, ta, ga, and fa. Then, the beginning reader is supposed to build on those small sounds to form whole words. Visual-spatials understand big picture information first, not the smallest details! Because VSLs think in pictures, they need to read in pictures. What is the picture of "ga"? Or, "the"? Can you create a mental picture of "the"? Do you realize there are nine different sounds just for the letter "o"? (Tot, vote, toot, book, ton, town, boy, pour, and lesson!) How does one create a picture for nine different versions of the same letter? Even more confusing is the use of "gh" as in tough, through, and hiccough!

When VSLs are taught to read by looking at whole words first, not the smallest sounds, they can make pictures for those words and

Figure 5. Student drawing of the word mountain.

learn them more easily. "Disneyland" and "xylophone" are easier to read (and spell) than "the" or "and." There is shape and distinction to them, but not to the smaller, simpler words.

Some words just naturally make you think of a picture because of the shape the letters make (like the letters "M" and "N" do in the word MouNtaiN; see Figure 5) or because of the meaning of the word. For example, see Figure 6, a depiction of rain that uses a raindrop to dot the "i." Your students probably can think of many more ways to draw words that include pictures. They can use different fonts that correspond with the word as described in the spelling techniques in Chapter 7. There are many words for which they cannot create a picture to represent: "an" or "the," for example. Your students can make a picture of the word by shaping it out of string, Wikki Stix, or clay. Some schools use letters made out of sandpaper so students can trace over the shape of the letter with their fingers.

Whole words can be placed on cards and hung from a key chain or stored in a special word box. Then, the beginning reader can practice sorting all of the words with similar starting sounds, similar ending sounds, or any other categories he or she can use to group the words. This is called *analytic phonics* and will help any reader improve his or her reading skills. There isn't always a single right answer to learning something and phonics certainly doesn't work for every student. For more on this, please see Maxwell's

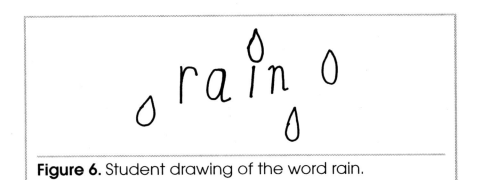

Figure 6. Student drawing of the word rain.

(2003) article, "Reading Help for Struggling Gifted Visual-Spatial Learners: Wholes and Patterns," which can be found at http://www.visualspatial.org/Articles/wholes.pdf.

Students, especially visual-spatial students, need to be encouraged to create mental images of what they are reading for recall and comprehension. Many of them have such difficulty decoding the words that they forget to simultaneously create mental pictures. A project in Escondido, CA, called the Mind's Eye focused on training students to produce mental images as they read. According to the program,

> . . . training students to generate mental images as they read can substantially improve reading comprehension. Teachers or aides show students how to identify key words which will help make a mental image and encourage the children to use those words to generate images. Gains in reading comprehension from this nine-week program almost tripled prior yearly average gains. Recall was twelve times greater than previous yearly gains, and while improvements in speed and accuracy were less dramatic, those scores doubled over the previous year's. (Pressley, 1979, as cited in Williams, 1983, p. 109)

If your students need help remembering the pictures they are creating in their minds, they should be encouraged to keep "notes"—drawings—of what they are reading. They can do this in the margins, if the book is their own, or in a separate notebook, if it is not. Critical information, such as the plot of the story or dates of information or names of characters they are studying, should be included in the drawings. I'll discuss more on note taking in Chapter 8.

In his book, *Gift of Dyslexia*, Ron Davis writes about a particularly successful method in helping emerging readers create mental images of what they are reading.

> Picture at Punctuation is the best technique I have seen for improving comprehension skill. . . . When they come to a comma, period, exclamation mark, question mark, dash, colon, or semi-colon they stop reading and tell me what they are picturing in their minds about what is happening in the story. . . .
>
> What makes this comprehension technique so good is it uses their strength of making mental pictures. I'm not drilling them with questions they might not be able to correctly process, I'm simply saying, "Tell me your picture." (from J. Ringle on the techniques of Davis, 1994, as cited in Silverman, 2002, p. 292)

Speed Reading

I have one huge tip for visual-spatial students about reading: speed read! Just like beginning readers have no need for the words "the," "and," "or," and so on, older readers aren't creating pictures for these words, either. So, they can just skip them. Teach them to practice running a finger, very quickly, over one line of words, then the next. They should jump right over the words that their minds don't make a picture for. Most speed readers use their index finger to race under the lines of text as they read.

Here's an example of how to skip pictureless words. First, read this sentence:

Then, on the following morning, Jody ran to the nearby grocery store to fetch a gallon of fresh milk for his mother.

Now, watch how much easier it is to read this sentence by skipping over the words that have no mental picture, reading only the words that create an image in your mind:

Morning, Jody ran store milk mother

Can you do it? Can you skip the pictureless words? Was it easier? Are you missing any facts from the first sentence? Does the sentence with much fewer words still create a picture in your mind of what the character is doing, when, and for whom? You don't even need the adjective "fresh" because you know he's buying the milk that morning. If you are a picture thinker, it's easier to make a mental picture when you don't have to stop and read the pictureless words. This technique won't affect comprehension because the reader is only eliminating the words for which there is no picture to represent, and were not going to recall anyway. It actually serves to increase comprehension because now, the student can focus exclusively on creating pictures for what is being read, mental pictures that can be recalled later with increased accuracy because he or she is no longer spending frustrating study time with pictureless words.

Reading for Important Information

There are plenty of hints placed in textbooks to indicate that the reader has stumbled upon important information. New words a reader is expected to recall later often are in bold print; important information often is represented in a graph, diagram, or other visual, as well as provided in the text; and subheadings often guide the reader for a good overview of the material.

One fun and effective technique for demonstrating to students how to be aware of important information within their reading is to do a "Textbook Scavenger Hunt" at the beginning of the school year. In a Textbook Scavenger Hunt, you ask students to seek general and specific information from chapters, the glossary, the index, and other areas of the book. The hunt through various chapters and other sections gives the student an overview of what the text covers and what they will be exposed to during the course of the school year. I've found it an excellent introduction to the material, particularly for visual-spatial learners, who can then make connections when new material is being presented. They'll remember, for example, that the class is going to cover certain aspects of the timeline in history because they visited that chapter, however briefly, at the first of the school year. Making connections helps VSLs retain what they are hearing and reading.

When I was in school, I used to fold the corners of any pages that contained names, dates, and other important information. Today, there are many great products available at office supply stores so students don't need to damage their books. Post-it® tabs in a variety of colors fill this need far better than corner folding. Teach your students to use different colored tabs for different information. For example, green tabs are for dates they must remember, blue tabs are important names, and red tabs are new words. Don't dictate what the colors mean; rather, let each student determine what color-coding system works best. The tabs can be stuck right on the specific line of text that contains the information. Show your students how to have just the colored tab area sticking off the page for easy reference.

A Final Note About Reading

For students who have difficulty reading, or who read slowly, consider incorporating comic books or fantasy books with lots of visuals. Perhaps books on something that really interests the child, a favorite animal or another country, or something appealing enough to keep trying to hone reading skills. You also might consider having him or her check out recorded books from a library. Being read to enables the student to learn the vocabulary and allows the visual-spatial student to create the mental images necessary to be able to recall the story in accurate detail.

Many visual-spatial children are late readers (Silverman, 2002; West, 2004). Some have difficulty tracking a line of print. My own son surprised his teachers and parents when he was randomly selected to demonstrate a vision-tracking instrument for his school. His comprehension was significantly above grade level and no adult in his life suspected he had a tracking issue, but it turned out that each of his eyes was reading a different line of text—simultaneously! Six months of vision therapy corrected this issue and usually does for kids with this problem. Providing books with a larger print size may be a consideration, as well. This often is easier on a student's eyes. Some kids find reading easier when they use a colored transparency, like yellow or green, and place that over the page. Finally, there are high-interest books available from Barrington Stoke Publications that are printed on special paper using a font with an extra half space between letters that has been proven easier to read for students who are dyslexic. You can find these online at http://www.BarringtonStoke.co.uk.

Other VSLs are delayed in their reading skills because they receive only phonetic instruction. However, most visual-spatial learners have a strong desire to read, particularly in their quest to learn how things work. You have the opportunity to help your beginning readers crack the code by providing visual instruction in the form of a whole word/sight word approach.

chapter 5

Creative Writing

AN aptitude for creative writing is one of the many gifts of being a visual-spatial learner. These children have a wild imagination coupled with a great sense of humor. They often come up with wonderfully elaborate, detailed stories. But, when it comes to getting them on paper, what they produce often employs vocabulary several grade levels below what you know they're capable of writing. For some, the challenge is in the organization of their numerous mental images. For others, the difficulty is in translating mental images into words and then handwriting them neatly. Some students think they will fail at the spelling, grammar, or punctuation and that causes them to freeze or underperform.

When a student writes, she or he has to synchronize letter formation (or keyboarding), spelling, punctuation, grammar, capitalization, prior knowledge, and vocabulary. All of these output tributaries have to flow into the main river at about the same rate. A budding writer can't have the punctuation arriving eleven seconds after the capitalization. Difficulty achieving the required degree of synchronization is one reason many students . . . find writing to be a form of cruel and unusual punishment. (Levine, 2002, p. 80)

I tell parents and teachers who are not visual-spatial learners to do this exercise: Imagine you are watching a movie that incorporates large doses of color, images, and emotion. Numerous pictures are flashing quickly before you. Now, stop and write down, in words, all that you see, feel, and sense in a logical, sequential report. Most people, even sequential thinkers, can't do it. Students often are asked to write all that they see in their mind's eye. If a "picture is worth a thousand words," and they think in thousands of pictures, how are they to find just the words needed for any story or report? For many visual-spatial students, it is an impossible task. Writing becomes an assignment they dread. And so, we see assignments submitted that don't even begin to include all of the details that were in these student's mental pictures, or what they were able to tell us verbally.

I have some tips to help your visual-spatial students successfully put on paper all of their creative ideas. So often, the visual-spatial student has a fabulous idea for a creative story, but shortly after putting pencil to paper, the student gets lost or halts completely, not sure how to proceed because the mental picture has been lost. For many students, it helps to draw out their mental pictures and then return later to writing the words that correspond to those pictures. When the pictures are put on paper first, it's easier to remember where the story was headed.

Allow dictation. Because images often flow faster and more vividly than visual-spatial students can write or type, allow them to dictate all or part of a story to someone else. First, they dictate the ideas. Then, they review their unedited ideas and edit as much as they can (with the help of spell checker and grammar check). Visual-spatial students should be encouraged to learn keyboarding skills early on, as discussed in Chapter 6, because typing, once they are proficient, will be a much faster means of getting their stories on paper than writing by hand.

Consider giving weight to other aspects of a creative writing project. For example, allow your students to create costumes, a storyboard, or a model to go with their stories and give credit to them for these efforts. Or, try any of the other ideas you'll find listed in Alternative Assignments at the end of this chapter. This will give visual-spatial students a chance to show off their talents in creating wonderful accompaniments to their stories. Credit for their extra time and effort can offset the fact that they often are unable to produce a written story free of spelling and grammatical errors. Please also consider grading the content of your students' ideas separate from the penmanship and mechanics.

Other Types of Written Assignments

Many visual-spatial students have difficulty with written assignments, especially reports. There are a number of alternative assignments you can offer that allow your students to demonstrate what they've read and learned. I've included a list of some possibilities for you to consider at the end of this chapter.

For starters, let's suppose the assignment is to write a book report. What other ways can students exhibit they have read and understood the book besides writing a two-page report? Thinking outside the box comes naturally for these kids; ask them to come up with projects that display their knowledge. What about a videotaped "Interview With the Author"? The student could research the roles and create scripts for both an interviewer and the author of the book, or the student could collaborate with a classmate to research and role-play these parts. The important aspects of any well-written book report (e.g., the plot, the main characters, the climax of the story, some information about the author, the inspiration for the story) would be included in this entertaining format.

It would be interesting to create and it would certainly demonstrate knowledge of the book.

Alternative projects that don't necessarily include writing can be remarkable in their ability to call upon the reader's comprehension and understanding of the literature. In the next example, for instance, the reader's assignment requires significant awareness of the details in the story:

> I expected Mr. Williams [English teacher at an all-boys' school] to assign [an essay] to his boys. After all, that's the way *Lord of the Flies* is usually taught, according to the many study guides available for this book. But that's not what Mr. Williams did. "Let's see your maps," he said. Mr. Williams had given the boys a very different assignment: prepare a three-dimensional map of the island.
>
> Making a map of the island is not an easy assignment. There's no map in the book. The island does have many unique features, but how to make a map?
>
> As these boys learned firsthand, you can use the book to construct an accurate map, but only if you read the text with care. For instance, in the closing chapter you'll find the sentence, "The sunlight was slanting now into the palms by the wrecked shelter." You know that the wrecked shelter is near the beach. It's late in the evening. Knowing that the sun sets in the west, you deduce that if the beach were on the east side of the island, it wouldn't be possible for sunlight to be slanting into the palms late in the evening because the forest would block the sunlight. The beach can't be on the south side of the island; if it were, the mountain would block the sunlight. Nor can it be on the north side of the island, or the forest would block the sunlight. The beach has to be on the west side of the island. (Sax, 2005, p. 109)

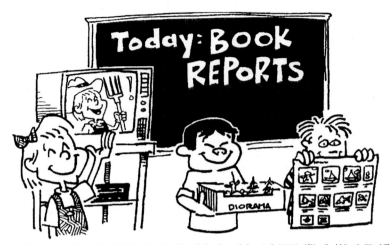

How about a diorama that shows the conflict or the climax of the story? What about making a mini-film of the main events? Or, perhaps a storyboard or a cartoon book? Can your students write a musical based on the book? How about designing a board game around certain events in the book? If the story took place during a specific time in history, can the student design costumed paper dolls to recreate the main scenes?

Now, let's suppose the assignment is to research a famous person in history. John Martin, formerly a popular middle school teacher at Rocky Mountain School for the Gifted and Creative in Boulder, CO, asked his students to select a famous scientist from the 1600s. The students were asked to:

- Draw a headstone for their famous scientist's grave. (This required researching the scientist's birth date, date of death, and writing an interesting, appropriate epitaph. It also included art.)

- Create a birth certificate. (This required researching the parents' names, and place and date of birth.)

- Create a timeline of events, including the scientist's contributions, as well as other important political events, inventions, music, and art of the era, etc. (This allowed the student to see what was happening in the world at the same time the scientist lived.)

- Create a business card for the scientist. (This required an understanding of the profession, the scientist's education and accomplishments, and finding out where the scientist lived or studied. It also included an art component.)

- Write a letter to a head of state (king, queen, president, etc.) requesting funding to continue research. (The student had to research who was in power at the time and produce a creative plea.)

- Write a newspaper article interviewing the scientist about his or her work. (This required an understanding of the scientist's contribution and its significance for the time period. It also could include an understanding of accepted beliefs or inventions of the time.)

There were additional parts to the assignment, but my point is that this teacher understood the importance of including activities that used both hemispheres of the brain to demonstrate what his students had learned. The research and writing he asked for meant his students had to rely on their left hemisphere to take notes, keep them organized, and write logically. The art, timeline, and creative thinking he solicited had his students using their right hemisphere to see the big picture and added fun and interest to the complete report.

By making the project interesting for his students, Mr. Martin was successful in turning what might have been a dreaded research paper into a fun and challenging project. It also was probably more enjoyable for him to review than old-fashioned reports.

There are countless ways that visual-spatial learners can show that they have read the material, understood the main ideas, and are prepared to report on their learning. It doesn't always have to be a written report. Any project that allows them to incorporate visuals, music, color, and/or humor engages the right hemisphere and calls upon their strongest suit. Allowing alternative assignments may mean some flexibility in evaluation on your part. Some of your students may be happy to produce a standard written book report or research paper, so you will not be comparing apples to apples if other students select a more creative approach to demonstrating their knowledge. I would encourage you to employ a contract (see p. 64 for an example) with each of your students that includes what format they have selected, either written book report or creative alternative or a mix of each, what you expect them to accomplish in producing their report or project, and the grade they can earn based on what they submit.

Report Writing

There will be times, however, when a standard written report must be assigned. Given the current status of the SAT with its timed essay requirement, it would behoove your students to be able to successfully organize their thoughts and create written output commensurate with their vivid mental images. To do so requires the visual-spatial student to begin with a lesson in organization. Visual-spatial students can discover successful strategies for creating written stories and reports: using a tape recorder or jotting their ideas in a web, designating colored note cards, or employing specialized software to get their mental pictures down on paper. Some of the kids I work with have no trouble telling someone everything that would be included in a report. It's the act of writing that causes them to freeze. Why not let them dictate a report into a tape recorder, then write down what they've said? They can play back the tape and add more as they write, but at least they'll have a starting point.

Webbing is a strategy of getting all of the ideas for a particular subject on paper, then building from those ideas. For example, suppose

Contract for
Alternative Assignments

I, _____, request permission to submit an alternative assignment to a written book report. The details of my assignment are as follows:

1. I will create _____ (diorama, board game, musical, etc.) to correspond with my reading of _____ (name of book title).

2. This project will include _____ (list all aspects) as a means of demonstrating a thorough understanding of the book.

3. The highest possible grade available to me, and what I will strive to earn, is a _____.

_____
(Signature of student)

_____
(Signature of teacher)

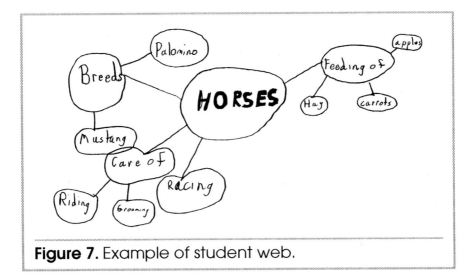

Figure 7. Example of student web.

the assignment is to research and write a report about a favorite animal. Teach your students to start the process by creating a web. Because VSLs naturally think about big picture ideas first, a web should be easier to create than a standard outline, which starts with small details and builds to a big picture. When they start creating a web, they should be allowed to brainstorm all of the related ideas that come to mind. No idea is silly or should be thrown out at this stage. A typical web might look something like the one shown in Figure 7.

It is standard procedure to request an outline prior to the writing of a full report. As teachers, many of us were taught that the first part of writing a report is to put down all of the ideas in an organized format. But, remember, visual-spatial learners don't think like that. They see the big picture first and then the small details, so writing an outline *first* is torture to them.

In the web featured in Figure 7, an outline would be created with the largest circle, "Horses," as our main subject. The subheadings would include "breeds," "care of," and "feeding of" with smaller circles branching off of them, such as "hay," "carrots," "mustang," "palomino," and so forth. The finished outline might look like this:

I. Horses
   A. Feeding of
      1. apples
      2. hay
      3. carrots
   B. Breeds
      1. mustang
      2. palomino
   C. Care of
      1. riding
      2. grooming
   D. Racing

If creating an outline from their web doesn't work, students can try using software such as Inspiration® or Kidspiration®, which allows students to visually create a graphic organizer using pictures, text, and spoken words. Or, students can write the report first and then generate an outline from the finished report. This may require some flexibility on your part, as students choosing this route should not be expected to complete the report in the same time others are drafting their outline.

The next step in creating their finished reports is to encourage your students to watch videos, visit related sites on the Internet, talk to a specialist (perhaps a veterinarian in the horse example mentioned previously), and read books to gather information on each of the areas necessary for the final report. They should take notes on everything they learn. The notes might be more useful to them if they write them on color-coded index cards. For example, in our example of a report on horses, they might use green index cards for any information learned about feeding horses, and they might choose yellow cards for the information researched about various breeds of horses. Keep in mind that notes don't have to be written words. If your students think in pictures, it will be more meaningful for them to take their notes in pictures. These could be actual drawings of what they have learned. For example, they could draw pictures of what horses eat, rather than writing the words, "hay," "carrots," and "apples." Hand-drawn images of what horses eat may be easier for them to recall than written words.

The final step in writing a report is to show your students how to gather all of their completed note cards. They should be in order by color so that all the information about how to care for horses is together, all the information about breeds of horses is together, and so on. The grouped cards should be in order according to the outline created from the web. The report can then be written directly from the note cards with all of the facts organized together, by color.

Proofreading

Another thing that makes my daughter different, I think, from her audio-sequential counterparts is that girls are supposed to be good at language arts. They are good spellers and writers. They tend to be good readers and quick talkers. My daughter isn't. Her spelling, handwriting, and grammar (in written work) is terrible. (K.C., parent)

When students begin constructing their written assignments, they should not worry about grammar, spelling, or punctuation. Each of these can be addressed once the rough draft is written. The first priority is to get the students' thoughts (pictures) into words and onto paper. After creating the rough draft, students should go through their reports first, looking only for spelling errors. If the report was typed on a computer, they should use spell checker to help, but they must be taught to beware of homonyms. Once they've corrected any spelling mistakes, have them go through the draft again, looking only for punctuation errors. Then, they should review the report a third time, looking only for any grammatical corrections. Don't ask your students to try to catch everything the first time they read through a rough draft—there's too much to look for and potentially have to change. Finally, have your students ask someone to help proofread for homonyms, missed words, and so forth. Even the finest writers have editors because we *all* need a second pair of eyes to review our work.

Alternative Assignments to Book Reports

- Videotape an interview with the author or act as a movie/book critic. Be sure to include a discussion of the book's plot, main characters, setting, conflict, and resolution.

- Build a diorama of the characters depicting the conflict or climax of the story.

- Create a mini-film of the story.

- Draw a storyboard that includes the main highlights of the story.

- Create a cartoon or comic strip version of the story.

- Compose a song or entire musical that includes a discussion of the book's plot, main characters, setting, conflict, and resolution.

- Create a board game based on events in the story.

- Design and create costumed paper dolls and retell the story.

- Create a PowerPoint or overhead presentation that includes a discussion of the book's plot, main characters, setting, conflict, and resolution.

- Design and present a puppet show based on the book.

- Create a journal or diary that the main character might have kept. This can be in either words or pictures.

- Design and produce a map that details where key events in the story took place.

- Design and produce a quilt of paper or fabric that includes key events and other highlights from the story.

- Create a Venn diagram that illustrates a comparison between the book you've read and another story (it can be either fiction or nonfiction).

- Create a mural or timeline for the story. Be sure to include the story's plot, main characters, setting, conflict, and resolution.

- Create a game show about the book (perhaps in the style of Jeopardy!) and act as the show's emcee.

- Prepare and present a mock trial where one or more of the main characters are defendants. Be sure the trial includes the story's plot, main characters, setting, conflict, and resolution.

Alternative Ideas
for Research Reports

Famous people:

- Draw a headstone for the famous person's grave.

- Create a birth certificate, including where the person was born and to whom.

- Create a timeline of events, including the famous person's contributions, as well as other important political events, inventions, music and art of the era, and the like.

- Create a business card for the famous person.

- Write a letter to a head of state (king, queen, president, etc.) requesting funding to continue research, exploration, or whatever activity the famous person was known for.

- Write a newspaper article interviewing the scientist about his or her work.

Animals, cities, or countries:

- Create an alphabet book that covers everything about your topic from A to Z.

- Design and produce a travel guide that highlights key historical events as well as places.

- Build a topographical map.

- Host a feast for your class featuring foods from the country you've studied. Dress in traditional costume and create a guessing game of facts from your country.

Additional ideas:

- Create a Web site, blog, or podcast that details all you have learned on a particular topic. You could include links to related sites, incorporate separate pages for various information, and so forth. This could be an individual or group effort depending on how detailed you want to be.

- Ask your students to think of their own creative ideas. You must be prepared to present the idea and defend how the project will demonstrate that you have read and understood the book.

chapter 6

The Art of Handwriting vs. the Act of Keyboarding

It seems her thoughts are there but her brain moves too fast and her slow writing makes the exercise of recording her thoughts unbearable. (G.T., parent)

NOW for the act of writing. Nearly every visual-spatial learner I've worked with has had trouble with handwriting. For some, their mental images come to them so quickly that their hands cannot keep up. For others, letters are multidimensional objects that rotate and roll around. It's tough to remember the proper direction of a multidimensional letter on a flat piece of paper. Still other students cannot form letters because they must begin in some random place

71

in space, as in manuscript writing. This proves just too daunting a task. (I often recommend that these students jump into cursive writing and forget printing altogether.)

One day soon, if it hasn't happened already, computers will be a part of every classroom. Then, visual-spatial students with strong right hemispheres will be able to put onto paper all of their thoughts, stories, poems, and notes to lectures without the frustration of handwriting. Why is the computer so important to their success? Because typing requires both hands to work together. This means both hemispheres of the brain are working together. If "two heads are better than one," wouldn't you agree that using both hemispheres, particularly the stronger right hemisphere for your visual-spatial students, is better than one? (Swimming, martial arts, and any type of physical activity that requires the student to "cross over" to the other side of the body are other great ways to use both hemispheres of the brain.)

The speed of typing, compared to writing by hand, allows mental images to flow faster, and the student doesn't have to stop and think about forming the letters. If you are able to flip and rotate letters in your mind, as many visual-spatials do, the letters p, b, d, and q are all the exact same shape in different positions. But, on a keyboard, the letters are in their capital form, so a Q looks nothing like a P, or a B, or a D, no matter how you twist and rotate that letter. Also, the keyboard doesn't care if you are left- or right-handed—you need both hands, equally.

There are plenty of keyboarding programs available for students, including Mavis Beacon®, Mario Teaches Typing®, Disney Interactive®, JumpStart®, Type 2 Learn®, and Typing Tutor® (Platinum and Gold editions). I've even seen keyboards and mice made for young students with smaller hands. Your students will be using computers throughout their lives, so why not teach them how to use them now? Learning to type on a keyboard may be the best way of completing homework assignments quickly and getting all of their thoughts down on paper. In my experience, once a student is able to type 30 words a minute, the jump to much faster typing speeds (60 wpm and faster) comes very quickly. Listed below are some excellent tips for students using computers:

- Lower the monitor for kids to help keep their neck straight. Monitors are usually situated for adults, so make sure they are at a good height for your students.

- Raise or lower chairs to help keep students' wrists and arms level with the keyboard.

- Always adjust the monitor to reduce glare.

- Have your students take frequent breaks to reduce repetitive stress injuries.

- Make sure your students know what a light touch is when using the keyboard or mouse. They shouldn't bang with their fingers as this produces more stress to joints and tendons in the hands, wrists, and arms.

- Help organize the work area around your students while at they are at the computer so they can easily reach items around them without too much strain.

- Have students get up and exercise a bit. Simple stretching is easy and can be done in a fun way to get them moving. Exercise will help decrease muscle fatigue.

- Try to help students notice the correct wrist position when typing. They may have difficulty remembering that their wrist should be level with the keyboard.

- Show pictures of ideal computer positioning rather than just writing or verbally explaining to them so they see the proper way to sit and maintain their arm and hand positions.

- Track balls, instead of a mouse, may also be a good alternative for student's smaller hands. (adapted from "Typing Injuries Frequently Asked Questions: Kids," 2007, ¶ 3)

Keyboarding and computer literacy are life skills for your students' generation. The next advancement will be voice activation. In fact, there already exist products such as Dragon NaturallySpeaking that have been designed for student use and allow the student to dictate to the computer. The latest versions promote use for students in grades 3 and higher and claim not to require voice training, as needed in earlier versions. (For Mac users, Apple Speech Recognition is available.) For kids who've been instant messaging, there is new software for Macs called TextExpander, which automatically expands typed abbreviations. When a student types "ttys," it instantly becomes "Talk to you soon."

Until your students become proficient at keyboarding, please remember to evaluate the content of their ideas separate from the quality of their penmanship. The creative part of the entire writing process is the single area in which they have a natural ability to excel and therefore should be graded separately from all the mechanics as well as the penmanship.

Handwriting as Art

If keyboarding is not an option for your students, then they can be taught handwriting as an art form. I would encourage you to purchase a set of calligraphy pens for your class and teach your students how to write beautiful letters. When they see the art in writing by hand, it may become a joy to create rather than a chore. Calligraphy should be taught slowly and with purpose, the way handwriting was taught a century ago, before the invention of the ballpoint pen. Take the time to enjoy this newfound art with your class. Take a look at the following examples sent to me by a mom in Australia. Her son's spelling test is shown in Figure 8. Note his teacher's comment, "I'm sure you have more of these correct, but

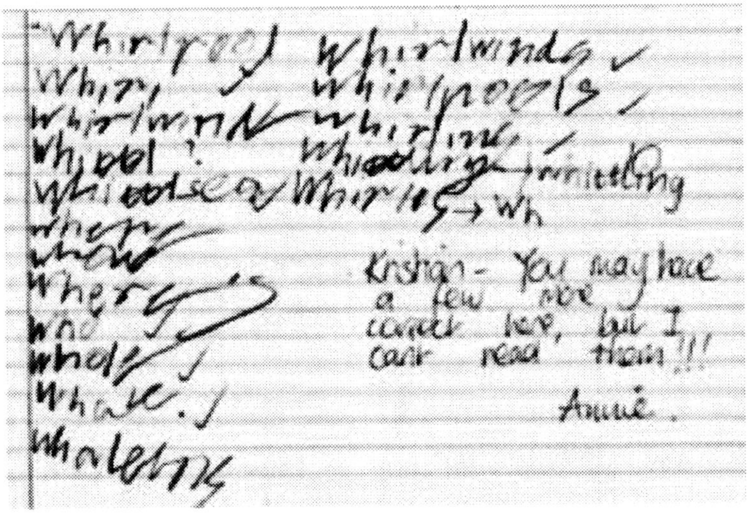

Figure 8. Student's writing on spelling test.

Figure 9. Student's writing after calligraphy lessons.

I can't read them." Then, after just 2 weeks with instruction in calligraphy, Figure 9 shows what the 7-year-old produced.

The ability to write beautiful flowing text will increase your students' confidence and legibility. Tip: It is a good idea to enlist parents' help when teaching your students calligraphy. Perhaps there are party invitations; place cards at the holiday table; birth announcements or wedding notes; even labels for boxes of toys, pictures, favorite things, CDs, DVDs—anything that could be created at home that would reinforce learning their new art form.

chapter 7 Helping Students Ace Their Spelling Tests

WHEN I present to audiences, I have a Peanuts© cartoon I use that shows Charlie Brown in bed thinking, "Sometimes I lie awake at night and wonder, 'What is the meaning of life?' Then a voice comes to me that says, 'I before E, except after C.'" I'm sure you've heard and probably used this spelling rule. Who makes up these crazy spelling rules? There often are so many exceptions to the rules, it seems silly to have the rule in the first place!

Many visual-spatial learners struggle with spelling (Silverman, 2002). Their gift is in creating fantastic stories using the vivid imaginations they were born with, but not necessarily in getting those stories to paper with spelling the rest of us can recognize. This chapter will help your students stay excited about creating stories *and* being able to spell correctly.

Like everything else these students learn, in order to remember the proper spelling of words, they must be taught to create permanent mental images of them. Without those pictures to see in their minds' eyes, they'll be trying to memorize spelling rules and all the times they are broken. And, they'll likely fail. So, how are you going to help your students create pictures of their spelling words?

First, have them draw a picture that includes all of the letters of the word. They can make up a story to go with it, if they like. Remember Figure 5 from Chapter 4 (see p. 50)? The student illustrated the word, "Mountain." The characters in this student's tale are climbing and skiing the mountain and the student made up a story about why the "a" had to come before the "i" because that was something he kept forgetting to do when he tried to spell the word. His story described how the character must first slide down the mountain, and then use a pick (which he turned the "I" into) to climb back up. Obviously, this approach of having a character on each letter may be a bit excessive and it's unlikely your students would need to follow this precise example, but it is still a good example of how this strategy can work.

If there is a certain part of a spelling word that is giving your students trouble, have them take a blank white piece of paper and write the word on it. They should use a colored marker and write the part that they keep forgetting in really large letters (in the mountain example, this would be the "a" and the "i":

Mount**ai**n

In order for the right hemisphere of the brain to remember an image, it helps to have students add color, size, or humor to everything they learn (Hardiman, 2003; Jensen, 2005; Sousa, 2006; Springer & Deutsch, 2001). When they truly have a mental image of the spelling word, they'll be able to see it well enough to spell the word forward and backward. As you prep your kids for their next spelling test, try having them spell the words backward to test whether or not they are ready. Or, ask that they prepare for the next spelling test at home by accurately spelling their words forward and backward.

Sometimes writing the letters of the word on stairs will help visual-spatials to see each letter of a word. They then can climb up the stairs, mentally, to spell the word backward and climb down the stairs to spell it forward! See the example below.

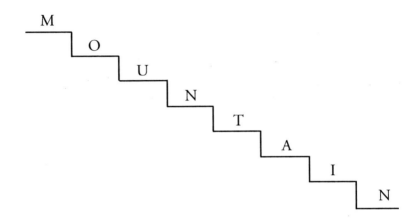

You'll find some reproducible staircases for spelling words that are from 5 to 10 letters long at the end of this chapter (see pp. 83–85).

Another technique that a mom in New Zealand recommended to me is to have your students type each of their spelling words on a computer using a different font for each word. They should select a font that matches the feeling or mood of the word. So, "serendipitous," which sounds like a fun and interesting word, might look like this: **serendipitous**. Or, they might choose these types of fonts for **FRIGHTENING** and *elegance*. However, remind students that they need to be sure to use a font they can read.

Many students have difficulty remembering how to spell the word "friend." Here's a silly story one student made up and he has since never forgotten the correct spelling:

FRIEND

"These FRIes from FRIday's sure taste good at the day's end!"

"You're right, FRIend!"

By using a rhyme and a double meaning on the letter combination "FRI," he used a trick that got his right hemisphere involved

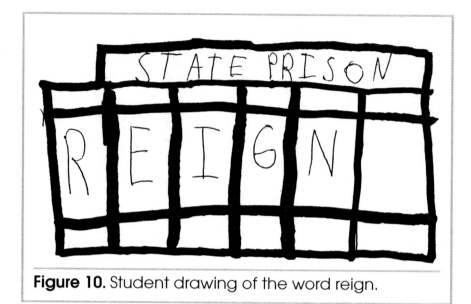

Figure 10. Student drawing of the word reign.

in remembering how to spell this word. Metaphors and multiple meanings of words are stored in the right hemisphere of the brain.

One teacher taught her students to actually put "rule-breaking" spelling words in jail, behind bars. The word was thrown in prison for breaking the rules and the image of the word behind bars would stick in the students' memories. Figure 10 shows what one student did for the word "reign" because the "ei" combination makes a long "a" sound. It breaks another rule by having a silent "g" in it.

Listed below are a few more strategies, borrowed from neuro-linguistic programming, that you can try to help your students create mental pictures of their spelling words using a visualization approach.

1. Have students write each spelling word in large print with bright-colored ink on a separate white piece of paper with the difficult part of the word written in a different color.

2. They should hold the card in front of them as far as their arm can reach, a little bit above the eyes.

3. Ask them to study the word carefully, then close their eyes and see if they can picture the word in their imaginations.

4. Now, have them do something wild and crazy to the word in their imaginations—the sillier the better. (They could make the word colorful, have the letters act as people or animals—anything that will help them remember how the word is spelled.)

5. They then should place the word somewhere in space, in front of or above their heads. There is an infinite amount of space around a person that can hold an equally infinite number of words. When your students are later asked to spell the word, they will likely look to the very place they "put" it.

6. Individually, ask each student to spell their word backward with their eyes closed. Was there an even rhythm between the letters? Good! That means they are really looking at a mental picture.

7. Next, have them spell their word forward with their eyes closed.

8. Have all of the students open their eyes and write the spelling word *once.*

9. They should close their eyes again and see if the word is still where they placed it in space. It should stay there forever!

Here's part of an e-mail I received from a parent in Australia who tried this strategy with her teenage son:

> So I drew up flash cards of 5 difficult words; inherent in their difficulty was they were not phonic, contained silent letters, or contained sounds that were not spelled phonically. I used: obscene, schematic, marmalade, machine, traditional.
>
> I sat with A & told him NOT to sound these out but to just put them straight into his "TV screen." He looked at

the cards—[spelled] them forwards/backwards and closed his eyes and told me it was done.

I asked him to spell the 5 words. My first shock was he [spelled] the 5 words correctly. My second shock was when he asked nonchalantly, "Do you need me to spell them backwards to you too?" I hadn't expected that and told him OK—where he proceeded to spell all 5 words to me correctly . . . backwards!

From a boy who could barely read and was unable to spell, I started to cry. He was spelling and spelling correctly forwards and backwards. He could SEE these words. (J.M.)

As I mentioned earlier, it is not unusual for visual-spatial learners to have difficulty with spelling, so I want you to consider this. Read the following paragraph. Don't try very hard, just quickly read the words:

Aoccdrnig to rscheearch at Cmabrigde Uinervtisy, it deson't mttaer waht oredr ltteers in a wrod apepar, the olny iprmoatnt tihng is taht the frist and lsat ltter be in the rghit pclae. The oethr ltteers can be a cmolpeet mses and you can sitll raed the wrod!

Apaprnelty, the huamn mnid deos not raed ervey lteter, but raeds the wrod as a wlohe. Ins't taht amzanig? So mcuh for the ipmorancte of spleling!

Now, I know that you were able to read this because you already know how to read and I'm not trying to suggest that a child would be able to read this. I just want you to consider that with computers and other tools available to your students, perhaps we are placing a bit too much emphasis on a proficiency that is not necessarily a life-skill for their time. The paragraph above is at least something to consider the next time you administer a spelling test.

Spelling Staircases

The following staircases are for your spelling words. To prepare for your spelling test, be sure you can spell each word forward and backward!

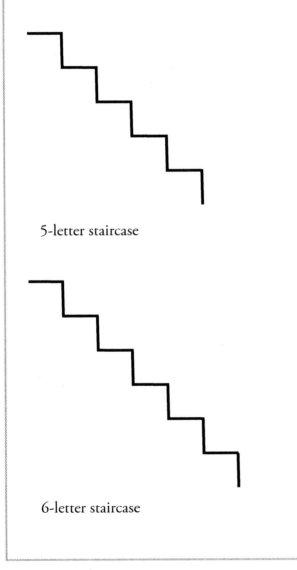

5-letter staircase

6-letter staircase

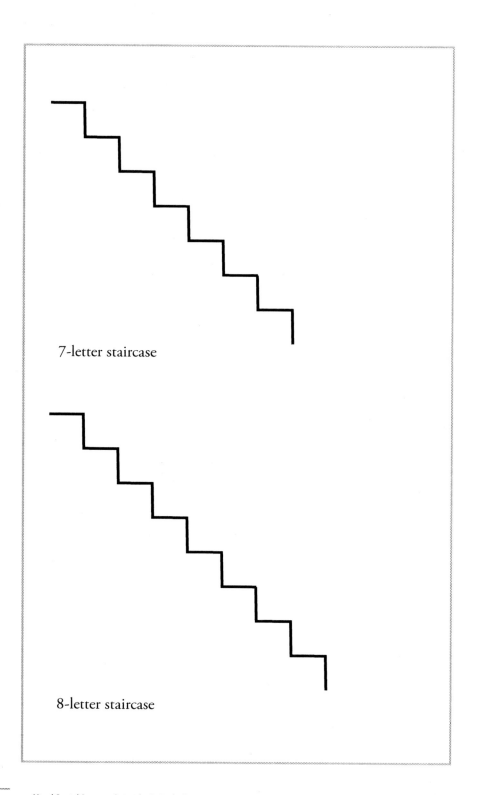

7-letter staircase

8-letter staircase

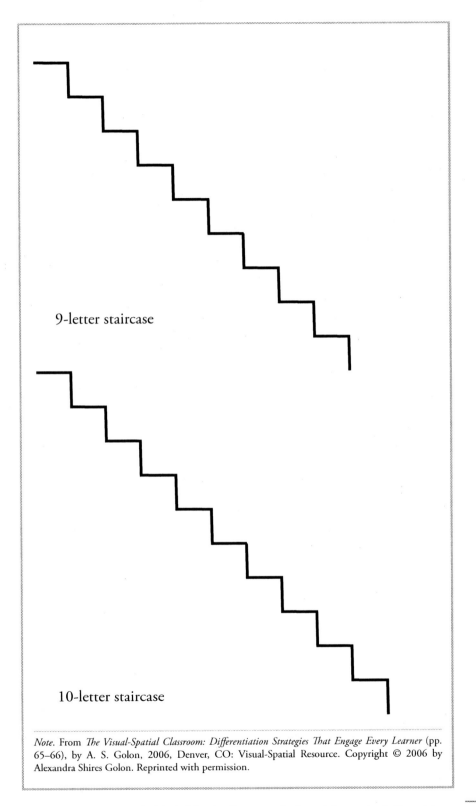

9-letter staircase

10-letter staircase

Note. From *The Visual-Spatial Classroom: Differentiation Strategies That Engage Every Learner* (pp. 65–66), by A. S. Golon, 2006, Denver, CO: Visual-Spatial Resource. Copyright © 2006 by Alexandra Shires Golon. Reprinted with permission.

chapter **8** **Taking Notes in Pictures**

The most obvious way of representing what someone has said is to draw a picture of it. (Ornstein, 1997, p. 36)

I mentioned in Chapter 4 that visual-spatial students should be allowed to take their notes in pictures. Here's a story from a student in a fifth-grade World History class that elaborates just why this technique works best for VSLs: One day the class was treated to a guest lecture from a man who had been in World War II. As the gentleman was giving his lecture (an oral presentation only, with no maps, pictures, or other images), he stood over one of the students who had dutifully chosen a seat, front and center. The lecturer noticed that the student was doodling in his notebook. He held the notebook up for the entire class to see and said, "I hope the rest of you are paying more attention than this young man." The student was, of course, horribly embarrassed.

After class, the visual-spatial doodler approached the guest teacher and explained that his "doodles" were how he took notes. He asked the gentleman to quiz him on any of the material. The guest teacher did and the student was able to answer each question correctly. The student had drawn the outlines of countries the gentleman had visited; he had drawn weapons the man had used from the descriptions given and he had engraved them with the years the man had visited there. The doodler remembered all of the new material because he had created pictures of the details, both in his notebook and in his mind. Pictures are permanent. The guest teacher apologized to the class the next day, saying he did not realize that students could effectively take notes in pictures. For visual-spatial learners, who excel in thinking in images, notes and other important information are better recalled when they are converted into pictures. When discussing learning strategies for all types of learners,

> The best way to remember something is to change it, to transform the information in some manner. If it's visual, make it verbal, if it's verbal create a diagram or picture of it. Use plenty of lists, tables, graphics, and other devices so that you're not merely sponging up the subject matter intact as it was presented. (Levine, 2002, p. 119)

Your visual-spatial students should be encouraged to use the technique of taking notes in picture form or creating diagrams while they are listening to a lecture or if they need notes on research material from a book, a TV show, or the Internet. Whatever source they are using to learn from, that material can be remembered and more easily recalled by drawing pictures. Drawing will help that material become permanent in their minds because they can later "download" those images whenever they need them.

Picture thinkers must be allowed to call upon their strength of storing and recalling images if we are to truly honor their learning style. *When you draw something, you own it.* As Williams (1983) noted,

> In another study. . . students recalled vocabulary words better when they read the definitions and drew their own

pictures to represent them than when they read and wrote the words and the definitions. Tracing a picture of the definition produced better recall than writing the definition, but *creating one's own visual image* was more effective than tracing. (p. 31, emphasis added)

A former student also recalls,

My 9th grade vocabulary teacher . . . had us learn 500 words in 9 weeks by using index cards. On the front of the index card, we wrote the vocabulary word. On the back of the card, we drew any picture that reminded us of the word. . . . To this day, more than 20 years later (!) I still remember almost all of those words. (as quoted in Silverman, 2002, p. 277)

If your students find that they can't draw fast enough while in class, you might consider allowing them to tape record the lecture. That way, they can complete their drawings later, when they can replay the tape and stop it as needed. It must be understood, however that recording for later listening is certainly not an excuse to zone out during class! I've included a contract for taping lectures at the end of this chapter (see p. 93) that you can use with your students, as well as a tape recording log for your own use (see p. 94). Some visual-spatial learners remember the teachers' facial expressions and precisely where they were standing when they discussed certain topics. Watching the teacher sometimes can work better than taking notes, when the student's head must be down, looking at a notebook. This may be particularly true for students with auditory issues. If a student has slow processing speed or a motor coordination deficit, he has to think about how to make the letters, which distracts him from focusing on the lecture.

If taking notes in pictures is too time consuming, your students can try a modified version of picture-note taking by combining a mix of drawing and words. Teach your students to use various sym-

Table 2

Abbreviations and Symbols

Word	Abbreviation/Symbol
with	w/
between	b/w
double	2x
triple	3x
On the other hand	OTOH
By the way	BTW
In the first place	1st pl
Δ	change
<	less than
>	greater than
@	at
Σ	sum

bols and abbreviations in their note taking. Table 2 provides some samples to get your students started.

Table 2 shows commonly used symbols and abbreviations, but your students also can make up their own. I have used ⇑ to mean something was increasing or growing, and ⇓ to mean something was being taken away or becoming smaller. The symbol Ω (Omega) is the last letter in the Greek alphabet. It could be used whenever something is ending or if a character dies in a book or play. The capital A is the Greek symbol for Alpha, or the beginning, and could be used to write about the start of something new, a birth, or the introduction of a new character. Students could use "B4" for the word "before," or "oppty" for "opportunity." Your students can think of numerous abbreviations that are meaningful to them and then start including them in their note taking.

I've used the abbreviation VSLs throughout this book to stand for visual-spatial learners. Many people abbreviate TV for television. If your students use Instant Messaging, they already know many acronyms that are used to type secret messages their parents don't know about (or so they think!). Acronyms also are used to keep the sender from having to type every word. Some of these include PLOS for Parents Looking Over Shoulder and LOL for Laughing Out Loud. Encourage your students to create their own acronyms in their note taking. Depending on the subject in which they are taking notes, there usually are commonly repeated phrases that they could substitute with an acronym.

Taking notes in pictures also works well for information your students have to research or memorize. For example, let's suppose you are studying the capitals of each state in the U.S. and your students learn that Salt Lake City is the capital of Utah, or that Springfield is the capital Illinois. Obviously, these are easy ones to create pictures for, but you get the point! Figure 11 shows what one student drew for me. Because he created his own drawing and he used humor, he is more likely to remember this capital than trying to just memorize it. Your students can do the same thing.

Another trick that works for many visual-spatial students is to create images of the words they are studying by boxing, circling, or underlining them. The simple act of having a particular word stand out from the others, by being enclosed or differentiated somehow, should help to create an image of the word.

Conclusion

Just as there is more than one way for visual-spatial students to master reading, writing, and arithmetic, there is more than the traditional word-only method for them to take notes of new information. Going beyond granting permission for students to draw and actually instructing your VSL students in how to create effective

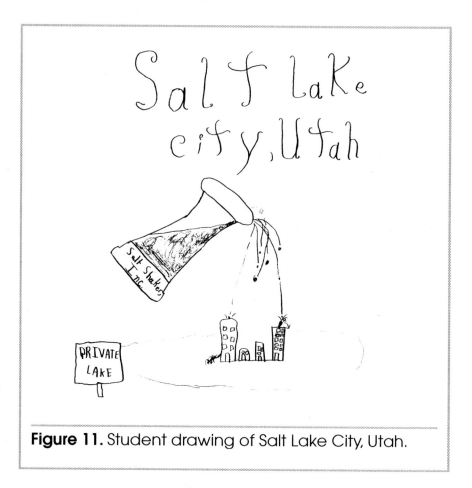

Figure 11. Student drawing of Salt Lake City, Utah.

images to use as notes will allow them to call upon their strengths and likely will result in greater success when recalling that information. Like the doodler I wrote of at the beginning of this chapter, creating one's own images to represent new material can be a powerful, more meaningful strategy than relying on words alone.

Agreement for
Classroom Tape Recording

I, _____, request permission to tape record class lectures under the following conditions:

1. that my attention shall remain focused on the teacher/lecture,

2. that I shall be responsible for creating appropriate notes (in picture or word form) based on the lecture, and

3. that I will not misuse the recorder nor distract other students.

_____
(Signature of student)

_____
(Signature of teacher)

Note. From *The Visual-Spatial Classroom: Differentiation Strategies That Engage Every Learner* (p. 73), by A. S. Golon, 2006, Denver, CO: Visual-Spatial Resource. Copyright © 2006 by Alexandra Shires Golon. Reprinted with permission.

Tape Recording Log

Use this log to record those students under contract for Classroom Tape Recording and to monitor the effectiveness of this strategy.

Student's Name	Contract Date	Contract Initiated Because . . .	Behavior Changes

chapter **9** **Teaching Math Facts**

Illustrated by Buck Jones. Copyright © held by Alexandra Shires Golon. From Golon, A. S. (2006). *The Visual-Spatial Classroom: Differentiation Strategies That Engage Every Learner!* (p. 75). Denver, CO: Visual-Spatial Resource. May not be reproduced without permission. Used with permission.

IF you're using Mad Minutes or some other form of rote memorization technique to help your students memorize the times tables, I want to ask you to set those materials aside for just one week. If you'll try the tips in this chapter, I'm confident you can get every student to create permanent images of each multiplication fact that they can easily recall. Just try them! Visual-spatial learners are at a distinct disadvantage with memorization and timed tests because they cannot employ their strengths in any way that helps them succeed. Using images, music, and humor, and helping your students to discover patterns in numbers, will use the strengths of the right hemisphere and offer them an advantage at mastering their times tables.

Let's start by looking at the grid on the next page.

×	0	1	2	3	4	5	6	7	8	9	10	11	12
0													
1													
2													
3													
4													
5													
6													
7													
8													
9													
10													
11													
12													

Note. From If You Could See the Way I Think: A Handbook for Visual-Spatial Kids (p. 52), by A. S. Golon, 2005, Denver, CO: Visual-Spatial Resource. Copyright © 2005 by Alexandra Shires Golon. Reprinted with permission.

×	0	1	2	3	4	5	6	7	8	9	10	11	12
0	0	0	0	0	0	0	0	0	0	0	0	0	0
1	0	1	2	3	4	5	6	7	8	9	10	11	12
2	0	2									20		
3	0	3									30		
4	0	4									40		
5	0	5									50		
6	0	6									60		
7	0	7									70		
8	0	8									80		
9	0	9									90		
10	0	10	20	30	40	50	60	70	80	90	100	110	120
11	0	11									110		
12	0	12									120		

Figure 12. Grid with 0s, 1s, and 10s completed.

Note. From *If You Could See the Way I Think: A Handbook for Visual-Spatial Kids* (p. 53), by A. S. Golon, 2005, Denver, CO: Visual-Spatial Resource. Copyright © 2005 by Alexandra Shires Golon. Reprinted with permission.

I usually start by commiserating with the kids: "This grid is pretty big, huh? There are 169 facts in there. How on earth are you going to memorize 169 facts?" As visual-spatial learners, they're looking at the big picture, the entire grid. If they don't know many of the facts already, they're probably beginning to panic—169 facts is a lot of facts.

Start with the facts they know right from the start. Probably the 0s, the 1s, and the 10s, right? Let's fill those in. Your students' grids should look like Figure 12 when you're done.

Now take a piece of paper and lay it diagonally across the grid so that only the upper right half of it is showing (see Figure 13).

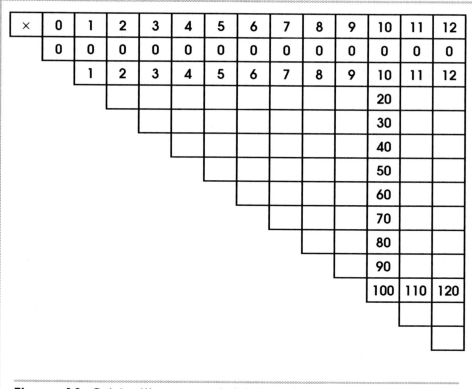

×	0	1	2	3	4	5	6	7	8	9	10	11	12
0	0	0	0	0	0	0	0	0	0	0	0	0	0
1		1	2	3	4	5	6	7	8	9	10	11	12
											20		
											30		
											40		
											50		
											60		
											70		
											80		
											90		
											100	110	120

Figure 13. Grid with upper right showing

Note. From *If You Could See the Way I Think: A Handbook for Visual-Spatial Kids* (p. 54), by A. S. Golon, 2005, Denver, CO: Visual-Spatial Resource. Copyright © 2005 by Alexandra Shires Golon. Reprinted with permission.

(If you have access to an overhead projector, copy Figure 13 onto a transparency to demonstrate this more easily.)

Demonstrate to your students that every number on the half of the grid that is showing has a matching number in the half that is covered. Tell them that this is known as the commutative principle. In algebra, it is shown as a * b = b * a. Or, 10 × 3 is the same as 3 × 10. The grid just got a whole lot smaller! They only have to learn half of it. (And your students just learned some algebra without even trying! The kids I've worked with love knowing they're learning algebra already.)

x	0	1	2	3	4	5	6	7	8	9	10	11	12
0	0	0	0	0	0	0	0	0	0	0	0	0	0
1	0	1	2	3	4	5	6	7	8	9	10	11	12
2	0	2	4	6	8	10	12	14	16	18	20	22	24
3	0	3	6			15					30	33	
4	0	4	8			20					40	44	
5	0	5	10	15	20	25	30	35	40	45	50	55	60
6	0	6	12			30					60	66	
7	0	7	14			35					70	77	
8	0	8	16			40					80	88	
9	0	9	18			45					90	99	
10	0	10	20	30	40	50	60	70	80	90	100	110	120
11	0	11	22	33	44	55	66	77	88	99	110		
12	0	12	24			60					120		

Figure 14. Grid with 2s and 5s added.

Note. From *If You Could See the Way I Think: A Handbook for Visual-Spatial Kids* (p. 55), by A. S. Golon, 2005, Denver, CO: Visual-Spatial Resource. Copyright © 2005 by Alexandra Shires Golon. Reprinted with permission.

I think the next easiest number to multiply by is probably 11. Have your kids fill in the rows for the 11s, up to 11 × 10, on the grid. I have some fun tricks for 11 × 11 and 11 × 12 that I'll share later in this chapter.

Do your students know how to skip count? Most kids I've worked with can skip count by 2s and by 5s. If they don't know how to skip by 5s, teach them that every answer for the 5s must end in either 5 or 0. There's a pattern to it, which their right hemispheres will love! Have them add those answers to their grids (see Figure 14).

Remember that one of the things the right hemisphere of the brain loves is rhythm—that's why it enjoys music so much. Here are some easy facts to learn because of the rhythm in the equations:

$5 \times 5 = 25$ $6 \times 6 = 36$

$6 \times 4 = 24$ $6 \times 8 = 48$

Try teaching these rhyming equations as your students stand and bounce, or jump, to the rhythm. Any time you can get their bodies into the act of learning, you've used another tactic of engaging the right hemisphere.

The right hemisphere also enjoys humor and tricks. These are simple ways to remember three more equations:

You have to be 16 to drive a 4×4. ($16 = 4 \times 4$, or $4 \times 4 = 16$)

5, 6, 7, 8 is what you remember for $56 = 7 \times 8$. ($7 \times 8 = 56$)

1, 2, 3, 4 is what you remember for $12 = 3 \times 4$. ($3 \times 4 = 12$)

Now, have your kids add these answers to the grid.

I think the next easiest number to multiply by is 9. There are so many tricks for remembering the 9s times tables, your students can pick a favorite. First, there's the finger method. What you do is assign each of your fingers a number, as shown in Figure 15. In the example shown, the equation would be asking 6×9, because the right thumb, the finger assigned as number 6, is folded down. That leaves five fingers up on your left (those represent the tens digit) and four fingers up on the right (those are the ones). The answer, then, is 54. Have your students try this with all of the equations for the 9s.

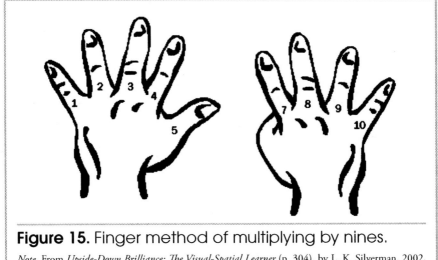

Figure 15. Finger method of multiplying by nines.

Note. From *Upside-Down Brilliance: The Visual-Spatial Learner* (p. 304), by L. K. Silverman, 2002, Denver, CO: DeLeon Publishing. Copyright © 2002 by Linda Kreger Silverman. Reprinted with permission.

If your students don't like the finger method, or if they need further reinforcement, show them how to look for patterns. The right hemisphere loves uncovering patterns, and the 9s have great patterns to discover. First, for every multiple of 9, the digit in the 10s column increases by one while the digit in the ones column decreases by one:

09
18
27
36
45
54
63
72
81
90

Next, no matter what you are multiplying 9 by, as long as it is between 1 and 9, the two digits of your answer will always add up to 9. For example, in the equation 4 × 9 = 36, the digits 3 + 6 = 9.

The last pattern I know of with the 9s is that all the possible answers have reverse answers. In other words, one possible answer is 09, another is 90, one is 18, and another is 81. Show your students the following pattern:

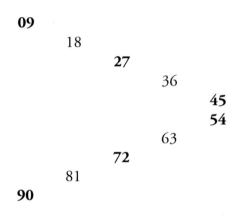

Now, have your students add all of the answers for the 9s to their grids.

Next, students can move on to the 3s. Borrow or purchase a copy of the Schoolhouse Rock multiplication video (http://www. school-house-rock.com/multiplicationrock.html). (These used to be commercials on Saturday morning television in the 1970s. Now, you can get them on video or DVD. There are even short cartoons for American History and English grammar.) The song they made up for memorizing the 3s is very catchy—your students won't be able to get it out of their heads! And, once it's in their heads, they'll be able to skip count by 3 easily. If you can't locate a copy of these videos, write the following numbers on a piece of blank white paper. Create your own rhythm (or have your students create one) for memorizing the order. It helps if you do this in sets of three (3, 6, 9, pause, 12, 15, 18, . . .) You may even want to sing!

$$3 \quad 6 \quad 9 \qquad 12 \quad 15 \quad 18 \qquad 21 \quad 24 \quad 27 \qquad 30$$

Notice there are three numbers in the ones category, three in the teens, and three in the twenties. Another pattern! Or, try having your students sing the 3s to "Jingle Bells":

"3, 6, 9   12, 15   18, 21   24, 27, 30, and you're done!"

Add the 3s facts to the grid.

Fours are really easy if you teach them as double the 2s. So, if your kids know that $7 \times 2 = 14$, then to find 7×4, they just split the 4 in half, take the answer to 7×2 (14), and double it: 28! Many students find it easier to take equations and cut them by half, then double an answer. Have them try this with the rest of the 4s. They can do the same thing with the 6s because 6 is just double 3. So, they should do the multiplication problem with 3 and double their answer. You can show this as the distributive property:

$$6 \times 8 = ?$$
$$(3 \times 8) + (3 \times 8) =$$
$$24 + 24 =$$
$$48$$

Have students fill in the rows for the 4s and 6s.

The 11s are easy up until 11×10, but what about 11×11 and 11×12 or even higher? Here's a wonderful trick for the 11s:

1. First, split the digits of the number you are multiplying by 11. So, let's start with the 11×12 and split the 12 like so:

1   2

2. Next, add the digits of that same number. So, in our example of 11 × 12, add the digits of 1 and 2 and place your answer between the split digits:

1   **3**   2

This works for any number times 11. Once you get to a number whose digits are greater than 10, students can add and carry. So, with an example such as 11 × 68, show your students the following:

1. Split the digits:

6   8

2. Add the digits:

6   **(1)4**   8

(Point out that obviously the answer can't be 6,148, so we have to carry the 10 over to the 6, making it 7.)

3. The final answer is:

7   4   8

Have your students fill in the 11s on their grids and take a moment to reflect how far they've come! The grid is nearly complete and should look like the one in Figure 16.

OK, finally we've reached the 12s. The 12s up to 12 × 9 are just the 2s plus 10 times the number you are multiplying by. So, if you're teaching 12 × 4, first have your students calculate 10 × 4, which equals 40. Then, have them calculate 2 × 4, which equals 8. Last, have them add the two answers, 40 + 8 = 48. They already know 12 × 10 and 12 × 11 from doing them earlier.

×	0	1	2	3	4	5	6	7	8	9	10	11	12
0	0	0	0	0	0	0	0	0	0	0	0	0	0
1	0	1	2	3	4	5	6	7	8	9	10	11	12
2	0	2	4	6	8	10	12	14	16	18	20	22	24
3	0	3	6	9	12	15	18	21	24	27	30	33	
4	0	4	8	12	16	20	24	28	32	36	40	44	
5	0	5	10	15	20	25	30	35	40	45	50	55	60
6	0	6	12	18	24	30	36	42	48	54	60	66	
7	0	7	14	21	28	35	42		56	63	70	77	
8	0	8	16	24	32	40	48	56		72	80	88	
9	0	9	18	27	36	45	54	63	72	81	90	99	
10	0	10	20	30	40	50	60	70	80	90	100	110	120
11	0	11	22	33	44	55	66	77	88	99	110	121	132
12	0	12	24			60					120	132	

Figure 16. Almost completed grid.

Note. From *If You Could See the Way I Think: A Handbook for Visual-Spatial Kids* (p. 83), by A. S. Golon, 2005, Denver, CO: Visual-Spatial Resource. Copyright © 2005 by Alexandra Shires Golon. Reprinted with permission.

Here's another way to teach the 12s. Ask your students to look for a pattern in all the possible answers for the 12s. They are listed below. (You may want to list these out on the board in one long column with a space after each group of five.)

00
12
24
36
48

60
72
84
96
108

120
132
144

If you look at the ones digit of each possible answer, it follows a 0, 2, 4, 6, 8 pattern. Each time the pattern is complete (at 8), the number in the tens digit skips a beat. Otherwise, the ones just increase by one each time. So, you have 1, 2, 3, 4, (skip), 6, 7, 8, 9, 10, (skip), 12, 13, 14. Using this method, your students can predict 12 × 15, and beyond.

Have your students add the 12 facts to the grid and notice how many empty boxes remain: There are only two facts left: 7 × 7 and 8 × 8 (see Figure 17).

Here's one way to teach those last two facts so that they're memorable. There's an easy sports trick for 7 × 7: The 49ers are a professional football team in San Francisco, CA. Below is a visual for how the players on a football team might be in position. Show your students how there are seven players in a row and that these are referred to as the linemen. Although each team has 11 players on the field for every play, only seven linemen can be at the front line at a time. So, 7 × 7 = 49(ers!). Here are two "teams" of players, represented by Xs and Os:

```
        X     X     X
              X
  X  X  X  X  X     X  X
  O  O  O  O  O     O  O
     O  O  O  O
```

×	0	1	2	3	4	5	6	7	8	9	10	11	12
0	0	0	0	0	0	0	0	0	0	0	0	0	0
1	0	1	2	3	4	5	6	7	8	9	10	11	12
2	0	2	4	6	8	10	12	14	16	18	20	22	24
3	0	3	6	9	12	15	18	21	24	27	30	33	36
4	0	4	8	12	16	20	24	28	32	36	40	44	48
5	0	5	10	15	20	25	30	35	40	45	50	55	60
6	0	6	12	18	24	30	36	42	48	54	60	66	72
7	0	7	14	21	28	35	42		56	63	70	77	84
8	0	8	16	24	32	40	48	56		72	80	88	96
9	0	9	18	27	36	45	54	63	72	81	90	99	108
10	0	10	20	30	40	50	60	70	80	90	100	110	120
11	0	11	22	33	44	55	66	77	88	99	110	121	132
12	0	12	24	36	48	60	72	84	96	108	120	132	144

Figure 17. Grid with only two facts remaining.

Ok, our final equation is 8 × 8. You can try this rhyming trick first:

"Eight and eight went to the store, to buy Nintendo 64!"

But, if your students aren't familiar with this older gaming system (Nintendo 64), try this: Ask them to think of something they *really* like. They can choose anything they like—from a favorite animal to food—it doesn't matter. Let's say someone chooses dolphins. Now, to master the equation 8 × 8, for example, ask that student to take a blank piece of paper and draw eight dolphins,

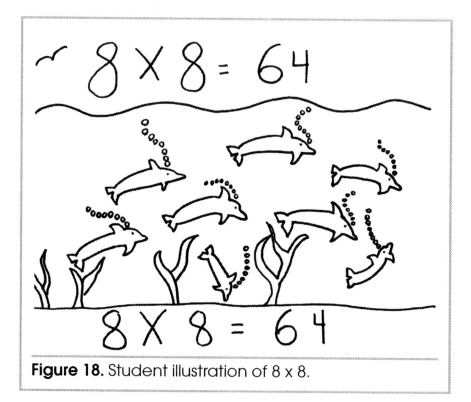

Figure 18. Student illustration of 8 x 8.

each with eight bubbles above their heads. Now, have the student write across the top and bottom of the paper "8 × 8" really large and in color. Then, ask the student to count all of the bubbles and place the answer, 64, at the end of each equation, on the top and bottom of the page (see Figure 18).

Send the illustrated equation home with the instructions for the student to tape the picture on a mirror to study while getting ready for bed, or above the bed, so that it is the last thing the student sees before falling asleep. Tell your students to make permanent mental pictures of their drawings, including the equation. They can replace the dolphins with anything that interests them; just make sure they have eight of a subject with eight of something else (e.g., pieces of pizza with slices of pepperoni, birthday cakes with candles, ice cream cones with scoops, donuts with sprinkles, squirrels with nuts, horses with apples, elephants with peanuts). In order for the technique to work, however, each student must have an *emotional connection to the subject* (that's why you had them choose some food or animal they *love*!) and they must draw the picture themselves, using no clip art or cut-out pictures. Remember the story of the doodler in the World History class? When students draw something, they own it!

> I told him to not try and "work it out" but to just put the "picture" of the equation and its answer in his head. Suddenly he knew 5 equations he hadn't known at the start. He could see "9 × 9 = 81" in his "TV Screen" and I was floored. He now sleeps with a times table chart above his head; first thing he sees each morning and last thing he sees each night and he is learning more of those all the time! (J.M., parent)

Your students also should use this technique for any of the facts that didn't stick with the other methods presented in this chapter. Be sure they use different animals, or other things they care about, for each equation, though. The technique won't work if they use the same image for different math facts.

The good news is that most students are able to permanently learn their math facts in less than one week when they use these visual strategies (and can learn them without the dreaded timed tests!).

Multiplying Multiple Digit Numbers

A lot of students, not just visual-spatial learners, have difficulty in multiplying multiple digit numbers. Many forget about using a placeholder; others fail to keep their numbers properly aligned.

Using graph paper so that there are columns helps some students, but I really like *lattice multiplication*. Although this technique was new to me, this method was first documented in 1202!

So, let's suppose the equation is 243 × 68. The first step is to create a grid and place the first number of the equation, 243, across the top and the second number, 68, down the right side, like so:

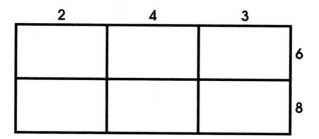

Next, divide each square in half, like so:

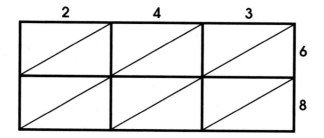

Have the student begin by multiplying the top left number (2) by the top number on the right, going down (6). The answer is divided with tens in the left half of the box and the ones in the right half:

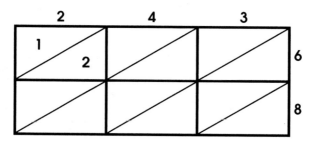

The student then works across to the right, multiplying the numbers as they intersect. So, the next set would be 4 × 6, again, with the tens digit written in the left half of the box and the ones in the right half. The following equation would be 3 × 6.

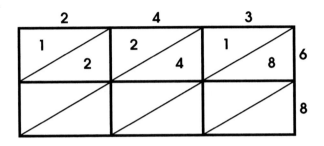

Once the top row has been completed, the student proceeds with the same strategy on the bottom row, 2 × 8, 4 × 8, and 3 × 8:

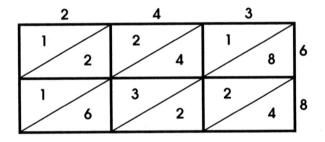

The next step is to extend the lines that divide each box and add the "columns" from right to left. Although this does include the counterintuitive step of adding from right to left, the need for a placeholder has been eliminated and results in fewer errors. The extensions should look like this:

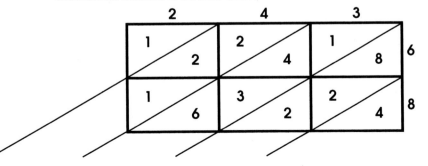

And, the added "columns" should look like this:

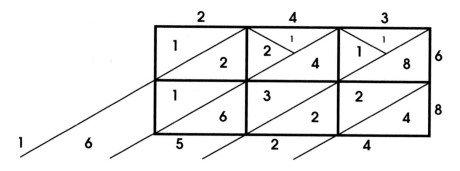

Yes, there is still carrying in this method. However, if carrying a digit becomes confusing for the student, the boxes can be divided again to hold the carried digit as shown below:

The answer to the original problem, 243 × 68, is 16,524. Initially, some teachers are concerned about the time required to create the grids involved for each equation. Take away the time constraints, or offer predrawn grids in advance, so that students can be empowered to complete the task to the degree that it is an important understanding of the concept—which is really all they need.

Division Is Just the Reverse!

. . . my 6-year-old [daughter] is giving me answers to basic division questions by "finding the times picture and going backwards!" (C.J., teacher and parent)

So, what about division? For a lot of the simple division problems (as opposed to long division problems), if your students truly have a picture of the multiplication fact, they'll be able to see the answer right away. For example, when they learned that, "You have to be 16 to drive a 4 × 4," they created a mental picture of the equation 4 × 4 = 16. So, if they were asked 16 ÷ 4 = ?, they should be able to see the missing number from their picture. When they learned 6 × 6 = 36, the picture of that rhyming equation should be clear to them when they are asked 36 ÷ 6 = ? What about the equations for which they drew pictures? If your students really do have that picture in memory, they'll be able to see which number is missing when asked the division problem.

Long Division: Showing the Work

Do your visual-spatial students answer math problems accurately, but rarely show any steps taken? Can some of them solve complex long division or algebraic equations, but not be able to tell you how they arrived at an answer? For visual-spatial learners, there are few requests more frustrating than, "Show your work." Because this type of learner intuitively grasps the "big picture" rather than taking what would be a painfully slow series of steps to reach a conclusion, the demand to "show your work" is nearly an impossible task. VSLs very often just see the correct answer—*and they're usu-*

ally right. They can't tell you how they know, they just know. They can't show you how they got their answer, they just got it.

Because most teachers are sequential thinkers, we teach in a step-by-step manner and expect our students to solve math problems in a step-by-step fashion. We also tend to anticipate that our students will be able to demonstrate their work by detailing the steps they took to arrive at their answers. The same is true for textbook developers and those who construct state achievement tests. This has had a devastating, unanticipated outcome for those who think in pictures and see the correct solution without ever taking a step. Every day, students are admonished, even accused of cheating, because they are intuitively able to reach accurate solutions to complex math problems but absolutely unable to explain how they got there. Most of the time, they lose partial or full credit for their answer because they did not show their work. At a time when "thinking outside the box" is a revered ability in the business world—being able to find solutions to complex problems is highly regarded—it's time we stop penalizing these students for their innate gifts and begin honoring what comes naturally to them.

Until That Day, However . . .

It is quite likely that visual-spatial students sitting in math classes at all different levels are being docked credit for answers they cannot support with detailed steps. "Show your work" doesn't have to mean complete the problem exactly as a left-hemispheric, auditory-sequential thinker would. It means, teach me, the left-hemispheric, auditory-sequential thinker, how you did this so I can do it myself. Show me, in the way I learn best (step-by-step), how to do this. When students know the material well enough to teach it, they really know it. If we help our visual-spatial students learn how to explain their answers to someone who does not think in images, then we've succeeded in teaching them to show the details in reaching their conclusions. Here's what one parent wrote about this technique:

> Dolls are useful. When E is having trouble with a concept, I have her "teach the dolls." For some reason the act of teaching the dolls helps her get things straight in her own mind and all of a sudden she "gets it." (K.C., parent)

Until we've created an understanding of different learning styles so pervasive that our state tests accommodate this learning style, we'll have to help our visual-spatial students cope with predominantly left-hemispheric tests. By teaching them how to communicate to those who do not think like they do, who do not immediately see the picture (or answer), they may be able to work within the system that unfairly docks credit due to them.

First, allow visual-spatial students to perfect whatever strategy works for them in solving their math problems. This is another opportunity to group students based on their preferred learning style. You can use the results from the VSL Quiz for Kids (see Chapter 2) to guide you in grouping your students. Have them test their methods with a calculator to be certain their answers are correct. Once the students have polished their unique systems, gradually increase the level of difficulty of the problems to continue to test their methods. Once they have consistently answered the problems correctly, using their own strategies, show them how to work in reverse. In other words, they can continue to use the method they devised (as long as they produce accurate results) to arrive at an answer and then they work backward through the problem to show the details to someone who needs to be shown the steps, or "work."

For example, in the long division problem below, let's suppose that the student, using whatever mental or written method this student has created, arrives at a solution and has proven it is correct by double-checking the answer with a calculator.

$$15\overline{)390} ^{26}$$

Now that the answer is known, the student simply works through the solution to show the steps. So, the first "work" to show is 15 × 2. This answer is then written directly under the 39:

Next, show the student that the next "work" to write out is to subtract the 30 from 39 and bring down the next digit:

$$
\begin{array}{r}
26 \\
15{\overline{\smash{\big)}\,390}} \\
30 \\
\hline
90
\end{array}
$$

The student doesn't need to figure out how many times 15 goes into 90, because he or she already knew (saw) that! It must be 6. But this step needs to be shown, so just write out the last bit of work:

$$
\begin{array}{r}
26 \\
15{\overline{\smash{\big)}\,390}} \\
30 \\
\hline
90 \\
90 \\
\hline
0
\end{array}
$$

While it may seem obvious to the student, the last number showing in any problem such as this must be 0 or the work has not been shown in a manner in which the auditory-sequential learner can follow.

By working backward through problems, in math and other areas, too (creating an outline of a report after the report is written qualifies as working backward), visual-spatial learners can demonstrate the steps of their work. Then, the auditory-sequential learners they must communicate with (primarily, teachers) can understand exactly how these students arrived at their answers. We open the doors by allowing them to work backward. Demonstrating their work in a manner that can be interpreted by sequential thinkers, visual-spatial learners can finally receive grades commensurate with their abilities.

If your students have difficulty keeping their numbers lined up correctly when doing division, try having them turn lined paper sideways so they have columns to place the numbers in. Or, they can use graph paper to help keep numbers aligned.

Using Math Manipulatives

There are lots of great products for "seeing" how math works and they're not limited to younger grades, either. Cuisenaire rods (available from http://www.etacuisenaire.com and most teacher supply stores) can be used to demonstrate math problems, from simple addition and subtraction, to algebraic equations. Borenson and Associates produce a great set of manipulatives for understanding algebra called Hands-On Equations® (see http://www.borenson.com for more information). You use a visual balance to shift parts of an equation to one side or another and then solve for a solution, or "x." By maintaining balance, literally, your students can see how algebra works. Look for or create more ways to *show* math and you'll engage every learner in your room. Check out "Ms. Math," Rachel McAnallen (see http://members.aol.com/pigonmath/page4.html), for great ideas on presenting math concepts, from number awareness, to higher level mathematics.

If your students are having trouble learning a particular math concept, find or make manipulatives you can use so they can *see* the math. Once they have a picture of how math works, many will understand the importance and enjoy the fun that can be found in this subject. The problem comes when students aren't given a chance to use something hands-on to watch how an equation comes together. They literally can't see how it happens and are turned off to math, sometimes permanently or until higher level mathematics is made available to them.

Turning students off to math is not a risk we can continue to take. As Kathryn Wallace (2005) pointed out in her article, "America's Brain Drain Crisis," "A 2003 survey of math and science literacy ranked American 15-year-olds against kids from other industrialized nations. In math, our students came in 24th out of 28 countries . . ." Wallace noted that, as a nation, losing our competitive edge in math will result in losing our global edge in science, engineering, invention, and, ultimately, our position as a world leader. Because most visual-spatial students are capable of multidimensional thinking, of understanding and predicting patterns, and of seeing whole concepts quickly, they are likely to excel in higher level mathematics leading to successful careers in math, science, engineering, architecture, and more. However, instruction that focuses on memorization of rules, formulas, and procedural steps provides few opportunities for gifted students to demonstrate higher level competencies (Sousa, 2006, p. 141). As educators, we cannot afford to let students with these talents turn away from math, believing themselves poor mathematicians simply because they did not memorize the times tables as quickly as we believed they should have.

chapter 10

Using Visual-Spatial Strengths to Learn New Material

I have met so many wonderful, innovative teachers who employ a countless variety of visual strategies so that their students can successfully learn and recall new material. Many of them have been kind enough to share their ideas with me and I'd like to offer them to you, in turn. If you have a tip or technique that has worked particularly well with the visual-spatial learners you've taught, I'd love to hear from you. You'll find my contact information on the About the Author page.

Let me start by showing you just how easy it is to incorporate visual imagery into your lesson plan. Take the information your students must memorize and work together with them to create a silly story with it. I once met a very animated teacher and conference presenter, Jon Pearson (http://www.createlearning.com). Jon was able to teach the 13 colonies in fewer than 5 minutes by having his audience memorize a ridiculous story—in pictures that everyone created in their minds—of a Jersey cow named Georgia, on top of the Empire State Building. Can you "see" New Jersey, Georgia, and New York in this story? The tale went on to include all 13 original American colonies. After each line we repeated, we were told to create an image in our mind's eye and to make it as big and silly as we could:

There's a cow named **Georgia** (Georgia)

It's a **Jersey** cow (New Jersey)

She's sitting on top of the **Empire State** Building (New York)

She's singing a couple of Christmas **carols** (North and South Carolina)

Under her arm is a **Virginia ham** (Virginia and New Hampshire)

The cow is wearing a pair of yellow **underwear** (Rhymes with Delaware)

In its hoof is a **pencil** (Pennsylvania)

The cow is making a **connect-the-dots** drawing (Connecticut)

Of **Marilyn** Monroe (Maryland)

Walking down a **road** (Rhode Island)

Going to **mass** (Massachusetts)

Illustrated by Buck Jones. Copyright © held by Alexandra Shires Golon. From Golon, A. S. (2002). *If You Could See the Way I Think: A Handbook for Visual-Spatial Kids* (p. 70). Denver, CO: DeLeon Publishing. May not be reproduced without permission. Used with permission.

When Jon was done, every member of the audience could remember the ridiculous image we had created mentally of a cow on top of the Empire State Building. By doing that, we were able to remember all 13 colonies. I have used this example in Canada, New Zealand, and Australia to prove the point that anyone can memorize new material, even if it is completely irrelevant to him or her. Why would anyone in Canada or "Down Under" care about American colonies? Many of the students I work with outside of the U.S. are familiar with states such as California and Florida, but they easily learn these 13 new ones from the mental image they create. The best part is that you and your students don't have to be artists to do this. If you want the images to be drawn, not just imagined, stick figures work just fine. As long as the story is funny, it easily can be recalled later. Color and exaggerated size effectively engage the right hemisphere, too. You can use this idea to help your students remember so many different types of material, from historical facts to scientific principles and so much more.

Beginning piano students often are taught the notes of the scale as "Every Good Boy Does Fine" (EGBDF). Have you used this mnemonic for memorizing the Great Lakes?

H   Huron

O   Ontario

M   Michigan

E   Erie

S   Superior

In Canada, this is taught in geographic order as:

Super (Superior)

Man (Michigan)

Helps (Huron)

Every (Erie)

One (Ontario)

Many of us were taught the names and order of the planets within our solar system using "My Very Excellent Mother Just Served Us Nine Pizzas" for Mercury, Venus, Earth, Mars, Jupiter, Saturn, Uranus, Neptune, and Pluto. But, with the recent demotion of Pluto, this mnemonic has had to be a little flexible, so I suggest using "My Very Excellent Mother Just Served Us Nachos." It's funny, which makes it memorable to students (and adults, too).

Using acronyms and mnemonics with your class as a way to help them memorize new material is another way of tapping into the strengths of the right hemispheres of your students. Mnemonics is a technique that works with all ages and grade levels and should not be discarded as "too elementary." Wolfe (2001) noted,

> Using a keyword imagery mnemonic process, in which subjects linked the sound of the word to an image of a concrete noun in English, researchers increased college students' retention of Spanish vocabulary words from 28 percent to 88 percent. (p. 154)

Using Music

A friend of mine sent me the following note:

> I took an exhausting/exhilarating 16-hour reflexology certification course this past weekend. I was told that memorizing the official 47-word definition of reflexology—exactly, word for word, was worth 15 points on the Certification exam. First I thought, I can never do this. Then, I decided I would make a song out of it!! I put it to a familiar tune! THAT came from YOU!! (E. Meckstroth, personal communication, October, 2004)

Catchy tunes are yet another strategy to make new information easy to remember and permanent. Take a common song, especially a nursery rhyme like "Three Blind Mice," "Twinkle, Twinkle Little Star," or "Happy Birthday," and put the information you are trying to teach your kids into that familiar melody. After all, 3-year-olds manage to learn 26 bits of completely irrelevant information (the alphabet) in proper order by putting the letters to music. Because the right hemisphere of the brain enjoys music, humor, and rhythm, your students will have a better chance of remembering new information if you do something silly with it. Try it—you may be surprised at the results!

Using Fantasy

Fantasy is a powerful form of visual thinking and is particularly useful when teaching about subjects that your students cannot experience firsthand. For example,

> A fantasy in which students imagine themselves either as a membrane or as a molecule passing through a membrane creates inner imagery which is useful to visual thinkers and provides concrete experience that has the power to stimulate and involve . . . (Williams, 1983, p. 32)

You can use fantasy, simulation, and role-playing to teach your students in a number of different areas, particularly science and social studies. Reenactments of significant historical periods help to secure new knowledge and make learning fun; imaginary travel to faraway places—even impossible ones like microscopic worlds—allows students to envision what life may have been like through another's eyes or as another form. "One of the more dramatic examples of the power of this type of thinking, Albert Einstein's fantasy of himself riding a ray of light, played an important role in the discovery of the theory of relativity" (Williams, 1983, p. 117). Classroom use of fantasy should incorporate plenty of time for students to create their images and encouragement for them to pursue this way of learning. It should be devoid of any preconceived notions of how one should create and experience the fantasy. One child's fantasy of life as a certain species of animal or of traveling to Ancient China will be quite unlike another's. This is a technique that every student will enjoy and one that your visual-spatial students will find to be a successful strategy in creating and recalling permanent images.

Using Metaphors

. . . there is far too little effort *connecting what is learned to the experience of the learner*—that is, putting the information in relevant context. (Ornstein, 1997, p. 171)

Helping students see connections between what they know and understand and something new they are learning, even though the two may appear completely unrelated, can facilitate that learning and help it become permanent. "If there's no connection to the learner's experience, the information gets lost and becomes just another meaningless memorization ritual" (Ornstein, 1997, p. 171). Working with metaphors can be a powerful strategy to aid students in making connections.

Here is an example of how this strategy can be used. The performance of a car is very much like that of the human body. The car makes use of a pump to distribute the fuel needed for movement, and the body uses a specialized heart. The car's fuel is gasoline, the body's is food; a car utilizes filters just as the body has an entire waste system, including kidneys; and the car releases exhaust, just as the human body rids itself of waste.

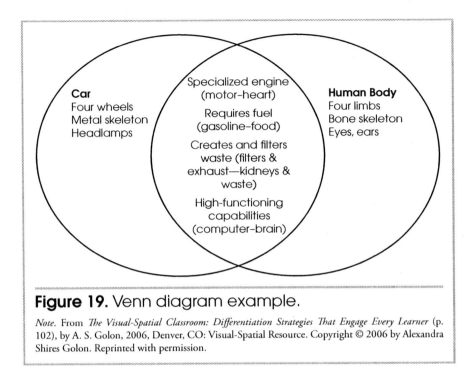

Figure 19. Venn diagram example.

Note. From *The Visual-Spatial Classroom: Differentiation Strategies That Engage Every Learner* (p. 102), by A. S. Golon, 2006, Denver, CO: Visual-Spatial Resource. Copyright © 2006 by Alexandra Shires Golon. Reprinted with permission.

With a little imagination, you can create metaphors for almost every subject you teach. When new material is presented as being quite familiar to something they already know, students can use that connection later to recall information accurately.

The real key is in teaching your students to use metaphorical thinking in their own pursuits. How is what they are learning this day similar or different to something they learned before? How does it compare to something they already know about? How is it like something from popular culture? Encourage your class to seek connections by asking, "Is what we're learning similar to when we studied _____?" By creating their own metaphors, students call upon their personal experiences, which they own and can easily recall. Using Venn diagrams can help in soliciting metaphors from your students. With a visual representation of how two subjects are alike and different, students often can take the concept and run with it. Figure 19 is an example of a Venn diagram using the same human body/car analogy.

One more note about using metaphors in your teaching and testing of new material. When material is tested in the same form in which it was presented, typically a verbal or written account of dates and places, students are encouraged only to memorize and regurgitate the information. They are not motivated to make any connections or engage in any new thinking. It isn't even necessary for them to understand what they are regurgitating, which is why we so often see that immediately following an exam, students can no longer recall the material. The information has been purged from their memories. Test questions based on metaphors, however, are an excellent way to evaluate comprehension. Compare the following activities from Williams' (1983) *Teaching for the Two-Sided Mind*:

List the major events leading up to the French Revolution and explain their importance.

versus,

How was the period leading up to the French Revolution like the building up of a thunderstorm? Be sure to include in your analogy the major events leading up to the Revolution.

A student might memorize the answer to the first question, but not the second. The analogy question requires that students not only know the events leading up to the Revolution but understand them well enough to explain their significance in terms of something else, in this case, a thunderstorm. (p. 71)

Make Learning Fun!

Another strategy you can use to remember information that has related pieces is to create a game of the material. This works great for memorizing capitals of states, countries of continents, specific animals of a species, or any other material that includes two groups of information that are related to each other. Matching games like Concentration (some people call it Memory) don't take long to make and you can solicit your students' help. Plus, they're fun to play! Just find some blank white index cards for recording your information. You can make each note card with words or drawings, whatever works best for you. Let's suppose your students are trying to memorize the state capitals. They should make a card for every state. They might use an outline of the state with the name included somewhere on or above the outline of it. Then, they should make a card for every capital. Have fun together making up silly stories if that helps them remember the names of the capitals. Remember the drawing of Salt Lake City, UT, on p. 92? Your students should use the same strategy to remember as many capitals and states as they can.

You also can use color to help students remember which capitals go with which states. Just have them include color in their drawings or put a dot of color somewhere on the state card and the same color dot on the card for the matching capital card. This will be a good way to make sure their answers are correct while they play the game, too.

Once all of the cards have been created, lay them face down and play the traditional game of Concentration, matching capital to state. (You'll probably want to start with just five or seven states and their capitals and gradually increase the number.) Students need to lay out (upside down) several cards with capitals, and then several cards with states. They should turn two cards over, and a match of a

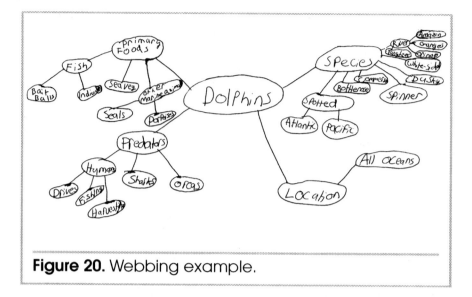

Figure 20. Webbing example.

state and its capital means the student collects the cards. If there's no match, the student should turn the cards back over and start again.

Here's one more idea to help you reinforce new information. In Chapter 5, I wrote about having students create webs of information to help organize their thoughts and notes before writing reports. They can use webbing to help remember new material, too. For example, let's say that in science class, your students have been studying dolphins. They are going to create reports and then give oral presentations on everything they have studied. They'll need to remember certain species, what they eat, where they live, and what predators they face. The webbing, or notes, for this topic might look something like what one student did, shown in Figure 20.

When students create a web that shows how the information is connected, they will have made a permanent mental picture of all of the facts about the subject. They won't have to spend a lot of time memorizing notes, only the pictures they created.

More Use of Pictures

When students have difficulty with something you are presenting, try having them draw what they do understand. Visual-spatial students may be better able to draw what they know and then see how to fill in the blanks than they are able to discuss with you. Often, when visualizing an image, they may have trouble translating the gaps into questions. Their drawings can be in the form of diagrams, maps, structures, or illustrations that communicate their understanding to a certain point—it just depends on what they're studying and how much they grasp so far.

Any time you encourage your students, whether they're visual-spatial *or* auditory-sequential, to incorporate images—those they draw, diagram, or mentally create—you've increased the likelihood they will retain new information permanently.

chapter 11 Organizational Skills

SEQUENTIAL   SPATIAL

MOST, if not all, visual-spatial learners are accused of being hopelessly unorganized. But, it has been my experience that many VSLs can find a needle in a haystack. I know of VSL kids, for example, with an uncanny ability to locate just the perfect LEGO™ piece even though their bedrooms or play areas may look as though a tornado has hit them!

It is important to note in the illustration above that, as long as each person is able to find exactly what he or she needs, in a reasonable amount of time, then neither one's method of organization is better than the other's. This is an area where "to each his own" is the rule. If visual-spatial students (like the person on the right in the illustration) were forced to "organize" the way the person on the left has done, they likely would never find another document again. The new system of organization would be completely foreign and these students would no longer be able to *see* just where every item is located.

However, if your VSL students find that they are losing important paperwork, notebooks, pencils, or anything else, they need to develop a better system. The new method must be their own, though. It simply will not work for the student to become organized under somebody else's system. If you think green folders are what students should use for science work, but green is meaningless to your students for remembering science, that will not be effective. You then can supply each student with the appropriate folders, files, colored envelopes and index cards, Post-it® Notes, or other organization tools to help them start getting organized. If your classroom budget doesn't allow you to purchase these types of supply items, ask your students to visit office supply stores at the beginning of the school year and include what they'll need in the classroom on their supply lists.

There's a reason why so many organizational products have come on the market in recent years. They must be the inventions of visual-spatials to help themselves and others who think and learn like they do. Your students also can use color for specific topics within a subject. For example, within a student's study of history, a single color can be used to take notes (on colored note cards) or highlight text (with colored Post-it® Notes) for each category of information he or she is to learn, including important dates, people, events, locations, and so forth. You'll find a Color Preference Survey for this scenario, as well as a blank survey for other subjects, at the end of this chapter (see pp.135–137).

Linda Leviton is a visual-spatial learner and a member of the Visual-Spatial Resource Access team. I asked her how she helps VSL kids get organized. According to her,

> VSLs are either horizontal or vertical organizers . . . if they are horizontal, they need a long table (preferably not deep) to put out (and leave out) works in process. If they are vertical, they need places to create stacks. I bought myself one of those paper sorters with cubbies and have it right next to

my computer (with labels for each section) and that's how I do it.

As for schoolwork, I have one word for you . . . pockets. Forget binders and putting holes in things. They need something they can shove papers into, and if you color code the pockets you have a better chance of the right paper getting into the right pocket. My preference is a folder with each class having its own colored pockets (one in front and one on back) . . . front is for current work or something to be turned in, back is for reference or past work. Just don't expect them to punch holes or get papers in sections that involve opening or closing anything; stuffing is what they do best! (L. Leviton, personal communication, May 31, 2004)

Using Planners

You read earlier that visual-spatial learners generally do not have a very good sense of time. These are the kids who wait until the 11th hour to start a 2-week assignment. Two weeks sounds like plenty of time, but then, the night before a due date, they're the ones who haven't completed the reading or the research! Show your students how to use a planner, especially one that offers week-at-a-glance and month-at-a-glance pages. They should use their planners to write down every important date, from field trip days to long-term assignments, holidays and other days off, even personal appointments and family commitments. I've found that having my kids write a due date for assignments 3–4 days before the actual due date has helped avoid last minute all-nighters. The extra built-in days allow time for editing, revisions, and a more relaxed approach to the deadline. Keeping an organized planner helps visual-spatial learners get a better feel for how long a "2-week assignment" truly is. The month-at-a-glance pages allow them to see how long it is until Christmas, the last day of school, their birthday, and other events they are anticipating.

To help your students (especially the "I'll be there in just a minute" kids) better understand the passage of time, I suggest using an inexpensive minute glass. You can find these as 1-, 3-, or 5-minute glasses or use ones from game sets. Set the timer up while they work or play, so they can glance at it and note the passage of various intervals of time. After awhile, they may be able to better sense when a certain amount of time has elapsed.

Creating Processes

"A place for everything and everything in its place"—this is not easy for visual-spatial kids, but it is a good tip that will last them a lifetime. Most adults seldom misplace car keys because many of us learn to place them in the exact same place every time we come home. Help your students create these kinds of processes in the routine of their day so that they can get and stay better organized. One process might include an inbox for all homework assignments located at the door so that as they walk in, it's the first thing they attend to, before they are seated. Another helpful process might be putting books and other homework immediately in a backpack or special folder to take home so they don't forget and leave those items in class. With a bit of trial-and-error to see what works and what doesn't, you can get your students organized and help them stay that way!

Name _____ Date _____

Color Preference Survey

What color do you associate with each of the following subjects? Use each color only once.

Red   Blue

Green   Yellow

Purple   Orange

Subject   **Color**

Math   _____

History   _____

Spelling   _____

Science   _____

Homework   _____

_____   _____

Name _____ Date _____

History Color Preference Survey

What color do you associate with each of the following topics?
Use each color only once.

Red   Blue

Green   Yellow

Purple   Orange

Topic   **Color**

Important Dates   _____

Important Names   _____

Events   _____

Locations   _____

Other   _____

_____   _____

Name _____ Date _____

Color Preference Survey

What color do you associate with each of the following topics?
Use each color only once.

Red   Blue

Green   Yellow

Purple   Orange

Topic   **Color**

_____   _____

_____   _____

_____   _____

_____   _____

_____   _____

_____   _____

chapter 12 Helping Your Students Stay Focused

You mean to tell me that you can do this complex math problem, but you can't tell me what day follows Tuesday?

Illustrated by Buck Jones. Copyright © held by Linda K. Silverman. From Silverman, L. K. (2002). *Upside-Down Brilliance: The Visual-Spatial Learner* (p. 29). Denver, CO: DeLeon Publishing. May not be reproduced without permission. Used with permission.

FOR many VSLs, some concepts and work that is really difficult for most people is quite easy to them, but often the material that other kids catch onto quickly is really tough for them. This is because challenging new material flips the "on switch" of the right hemisphere of the brain. When your VSL kids dive into something that's new and interesting, the right side of the brain is suddenly charged and ready to go. They can't zone out or doze off if what they are learning is new, interesting, funny, or challenging. The right hemisphere has to stay in the act and it's happy to do so! But, the minute the learning becomes boring, or is strictly words coming at them, they might as well get out a pillow and fall asleep, or start pestering their neighbor. Ask a coach of any sports team whether the team will perform better against a weaker competitor or a tougher school and he or she will answer that in order to get the best performance from athletes, facing a tougher team will bring out the best every time. The same is true for learning new material, so leave the boring, low-level material in your desk and constantly raise the bar, increasing the challenge and your students' participation along the way.

Here's what I tell the kids in my workshops; I hope you'll allow some of these strategies in your classroom:

> There's some good news and some not-so-good news. Here's the not-so-good news first: There will be some class or lecture or boss or *somebody* that you absolutely must pay attention to no matter how incredibly boring you think they are. Your grade or job or raise will depend on it. It's impossible to avoid such a situation. It's bound to happen. It happens to everyone.
>
> But, here is the good news: Every individual is in charge of his or her own right hemisphere! Each of us decides whether it's naptime or time to wake up and get in the game. The right hemisphere wants something more to do than just hold up the other side of the brain! So give it the opportunity.

Then I offer the following tips for keeping their attention focused. You may want to share these ideas with your students.

- Take your notes in pictures. Even if the notes are not required or needed, just draw images of what the speaker is saying. These don't have to be elaborate or even artistic; just get involved in really listening to the words so you can create matching drawings.

- Whether you're taking notes in pictures or words, use colored markers or an ink pen that lets you change colors. Use a different color each time a new bit of information is introduced or each time a different subject is mentioned. Using color will help you to remember the notes if you are quizzed later. You'll be able to see the notes, rather than trying to remember the words.

- Make a movie in your mind of what is being said. Closing your eyes in class may not be a good idea, but try to get enough information from the lecture so you can create a movie from it. Then, you can rewind your movie and play it over and over.

- Try doodling to keep you focused, even if the doodles don't have anything to do with what you are listening to. Sometimes the simple act of doodling is enough to keep your attention focused on what the speaker is saying.

- Bring a small object to fidget with while you are listening. A hacky sack or stress ball might work, or a balloon filled with a flour-sugar mix (and tightly sealed!), or any other small, easily manipulated object you can find. Just don't let it distract you and don't bother anybody else with it. Use it only to help you concentrate on the words of the lecture so that you can create mental images.

- Ask for an overview. The brain of a visual-spatial learner prefers big picture information first, so ask for it. Then, as you're listening to the lecture, you'll know where the talk is headed. You can take your notes (in words or pictures) in the margins of the overview, filling in the details from what the speaker says to match the outline given to you.

- Stay on top of the lecture by trying to predict where the speaker is going. What is the main point? What are the important facts? If you were to stand up and quiz the rest of the class, what would you put on the test?

Fidgets

Having a small object to manipulate, as mentioned above, often works to keep squirmy kids seated properly. I once worked with a class of fifth graders, most of whom rarely sat with all six legs (four from the chair and two from the student) on the floor. I convinced the teacher to allow each student to have a "fidget," in this case, a balloon filled with a 2:3 mix of sugar and flour. The rules for keeping a fidget were simple: No one can know you have it (keep it quiet and hidden in your hand), it cannot ever be used as a weapon, and it cannot be opened. One fidget was given to each student. The teacher was stunned to discover that they really worked. Just by having something small to massage in their hands, the students who before had difficulty remaining seated properly, were now able to do so. (The students who sat properly before the introduction of the fidgets—the ones who really didn't need fidgets—soon lost theirs or left them in their cubbies.) Toward the end of the school year, some of the students were able to give up the fidgets yet remain seated properly and only two students continued to use the fidget through the final semester. This is just one way you can easily accommodate the needs of the kinesthetic students in your class and it doesn't disrupt others nor detract from your ability to teach. I've included a contract for the Classroom Use of Fidgets for you to use with your students and a log to track its effectiveness on the next page.

Agreement for
Classroom Fidget Use

I, _____, request permission to use a classroom fidget under the following conditions:

1. that no one shall know I have said fidget (I shall keep it help quietly in my hand and never use it as a weapon or noisemaker), and

2. that I shall be responsible for maintaining the integrity of said fidget by not allowing it to break open or become lost.

_____
(Signature of student)

_____
(Signature of teacher)

Note. From *The Visual-Spatial Classroom: Differentiation Strategies That Engage Every Learner* (p. 73), by A. S. Golon, 2006, Denver, CO: Visual-Spatial Resource. Copyright © 2006 by Alexandra Shires Golon. Reprinted with permission.

Fidget Log

Use this log to record those students under contract for Fidget Use and to monitor the effectiveness of this strategy. The fidget is to be used to help the student remain seated properly and to aid in focusing attention. Record the reason for contract and any behavior changes observed.

Student's Name	Contract Date	Contract Initiated Because . . .	Behavior Changes
____	____	____	____
		____	____
		____	____
____	____	____	____
		____	____
		____	____
____	____	____	____
		____	____
		____	____
____	____	____	____
		____	____
		____	____
____	____	____	____
		____	____
		____	____

Note. From *The Visual-Spatial Classroom: Differentiation Strategies That Engage Every Learner* (p. 120), by A. S. Golon, 2006, Denver, CO: Visual-Spatial Resource. Copyright © 2006 by Alexandra Shires Golon. Reprinted with permission.

Doodling

Doodling is another effective way for visual-spatial students to stay focused on what they are hearing. The doodles don't have to be related to what they are listening to; just concentrating on what they are drawing helps many students retain what they are hearing. Allow your students to doodle as long as they adhere to the terms of the contract included on the following page. If you track the success of their recall when they are allowed to use this technique on the log that follows the Doodling Contract, I think you'll be surprised. As with the fidgets, the kids who don't need to doodle to focus will quickly drop it, but those who find it helpful will likely keep it as a strategy they use throughout their academic careers.

Free Movement

Another consideration for kids who have difficulty staying seated properly is to allow them, one at a time, to pace at the back of the room every so often. Initially, this suggestion is often met with complaints from other students, but eventually, as with the fidgets, only those who truly need this moment of movement will take advantage of it. I think you'll find that when you allow students this kind of freedom, it will not be abused and you'll have students who are better able to return to their seats and stay focused on your lessons. Plus, there is a substantial amount of research to support incorporating movement into your lesson plans (Gurian, 2001; Jensen, 2005; Sousa, 2006). The same area of the brain that processes movement, the cerebellum, is responsible for processing learning.

Agreement for
Classroom Doodling

I, _____, request permission to doodle during class under the following conditions:

1. that my doodling shall not distract myself or my classmates from learning, and

2. that I shall be responsible for keeping up with all required notes and maintain a passing grade in all subjects.

_____
(Signature of student)

_____
(Signature of teacher)

Note. From *The Visual-Spatial Classroom: Differentiation Strategies That Engage Every Learner* (p. 122), by A. S. Golon, 2006, Denver, CO: Visual-Spatial Resource. Copyright © 2006 by Alexandra Shires Golon. Reprinted with permission.

Doodle Log

Use this log to record those students under contract for Classroom Doodling to monitor the effectiveness of this strategy. Doodle contracts should be used for students who need help focusing. Record the reason for the contract and any behavior changes you notice.

Student's Name	Contract Date	Contract Initiated Because . . .	Behavior Changes

Note. From *The Visual-Spatial Classroom: Differentiation Strategies That Engage Every Learner* (p. 123), by A. S. Golon, 2006, Denver, CO: Visual-Spatial Resource. Copyright © 2006 by Alexandra Shires Golon. Reprinted with permission.

Visual-Spatial Learners, Copyright © Prufrock Press Inc. This page may be photocopied or reproduced with permission for individual use.

147

When we keep students active, we keep their energy levels up and provide their brains with the oxygen-rich blood needed for highest performance. Teachers who insist that students remain seated during the entire class period are not promoting optimal conditions for learning. (Jensen, 2005, p. 66)

Physical movement such as standing, stretching, walking, or marching can increase brain amine levels, which can help improve attentional focus. As a general policy, if students feel drowsy, they should be allowed to stand at the back of the room . . . provided they do so without attracting attention to themselves. (Jensen, 2005, p. 51)

The research also demonstrates a strong relationship between movement and language, movement and memory, as well as movement and attention. Here are some easy ways to incorporate movement in your class:

- passing the buck—toss a hacky sack or small ball to the student who is to answer the next question;
- take a group walk to "digest" new material;
- role-play, act out, and dramatize anything and everything;
- hands-on activities—find a way to get the students to "do" the lesson;
- incorporate stretching exercises as a breather between lessons;
- pair or group students in various corners of the room and set them to work creating jingles for information to be memorized (e.g., state capitals) or making up games with the material; and
- allow "walkabouts" for those that need more movement. (You'll find a contract for Classroom Walkabouts and a log for you on the following pages.)

Agreement for
Classroom Walkabouts

I, _____, request permission to quietly leave my seat and pace at the back of the room during class under the following conditions:

1. that my movement shall not distract myself or my classmates from learning, and

2. that I shall be responsible for keeping up with all required notes and maintain a passing grade in all subjects.

_____
(Signature of student)

_____
(Signature of teacher)

Walkabout Log

Use this log to record those students under contract for Walkabouts to monitor the effectiveness of this strategy. Walkabouts should be used for those students needing the kinesthetic benefit of periodic movement. Record the reason for the contract and any behavior changes noticed.

Student's Name	Contract Date	Contract Initiated Because . . .	Behavior Changes

Note. From *The Visual-Spatial Classroom: Differentiation Strategies That Engage Every Learner* (p. 127), by A. S. Golon, 2006, Denver, CO: Visual-Spatial Resource. Copyright © 2006 by Alexandra Shires Golon. Reprinted with permission.

chapter **13** **The Dreaded Timed Test**

HAVE you ever found yourself searching for just the right word as you're speaking? Or, the one word that truly matches the picture in your mind? This is precisely what happens to visual-spatials, nearly every day. The process for a visual-spatial learner to translate mental images into words (or numbers) is a lot like a computer downloading graphics. If you've ever downloaded a photograph on your computer, you know that it typically takes longer to bring up images than it takes to bring up text, especially if you still have a dial-up connection! Not only must VSLs "download" their mental images, they then have to convert them to words. When there's the pressure of a time limit, it can be particularly challenging, if not impossible, to do.

Timed tests are being seriously questioned. In fact, several states are moving toward untimed assessments. Mel Levine (2002) wrote in *A Mind at a Time*:

> . . . as kids get older, output controls function slower and slower and slower. In other words, well-controlled output requires adolescent minds to work slowly, to be reflective

rather than impulsive, to take their time and not do the first thing that comes to mind. This is ironic, of course, since our high schools force our kids to do everything as fast as possible. They have to write quickly, think fast, remember on the spot, sprint through timed tests, and meet tight deadlines. This frenzied pedagogical rhythm is totally contrary to what the students' brains are striving to become. . . . I think we should reward adolescents for taking as much time as they need to do a good job. Most tests should be untimed, or else students should be allowed to do as much as they can do well . . . (p. 84)

I have a funny story for you about my very visual-spatial son. One day, when he was about 7 years old, I was backing out of the driveway and he began panicking saying, "No! I'm not ready, don't go!" I called back, "What's wrong?" Matt hollered, "I can't get the backward seven to work!" I kept backing up as I was thinking, "Backward seven? What is it? How does it work? And, why does he need it?" As I started to drive forward down the street, the panic level in his voice rose and he began pleading with me not to go. When I finally got to the stop sign, I looked back to see that he couldn't get his seatbelt fastened. From Matt's point of view, his seatbelt was clearly a backward seven!

Illustrated by Buck Jones. Copyright © held by Alexandra Shires Golon. From Golon, A. S. (2002). *If You Could See the Way I Think: A Handbook for Visual Spatial Kids* (p. 83). Denver, CO: DeLeon Publishing. May not be reproduced without permission. Used with permission.

Because Matt could only see the picture in his mind and because there was pressure for him to tell me what was wrong (he knew better than to be in a forward-moving car with no seatbelt on), he could not translate his picture into words. He was left with "backward seven" because he couldn't find the word *seatbelt* fast enough to get me to stop the car. If you consider that a picture is worth a thousand words and your visual-spatial students are struggling to find just the one word that will match what you seek, you begin to understand the problem. It's not that these children are in any way slower than their auditory-sequential counterparts—it's that they're working twice as hard to translate their mental images.

Illustrated by Buck Jones. Copyright © held by Linda K. Silverman. From Silverman, L. K. (2002). *Upside-Down Brilliance: The Visual-Spatial Learner* (p. 282). Denver, CO: DeLeon Publishing. May not be reproduced without permission. Used with permission.

Such is the scenario when presented with timed tests. Most VSLs can't translate their mental pictures into words (or numbers, if it's a math test) very quickly when they are under pressure knowing they have a limited amount of time to get out the correct answer. They have an image readily available to them, but they are panic-stricken trying to translate that image into the right answer.

If you want your students to gain experience with timed tests, try some of the tips below to help speed up their translation time:

- Play games that require the players to answer within a specified time. Cranium™, Scattergories™, and Boggle™ are good examples of games that come with timers.

- Add a timer to a favorite game. Putting a time limit on Scrabble™ or Upwords™ provides practice in taking a timed spelling test. Adding a minute glass to Yahtzee™ may help with timed math tests. You can use a minute glass or quiet kitchen timer to limit the amount of time.

- Play Pictionary™ to practice translating words into pictures, then back into words. Add a time limit to the game, too. Charades is a fun game to play during which players start with a word, and then act it out in order to get other players to say the word.

- Games like "I'm Going on Safari" where players think of what they'll bring in alphabetical order give practice in translating images to words. The first player says, "I'm going on safari and I'm going to bring an apple (anything that starts with the letter "a")." Then the second player says, "I'm going on a safari and I'm going to bring an apple (or whatever the first player said) plus a beagle (anything that starts with the letter "b"). The game continues that way, through the alphabet. This requires players to keep words (or pictures they must translate into words) in their minds through the entire game/alphabet. Add a time limit to thinking up a new word and remembering the entire list.

If the ticking of a timer bothers your students, make sure you use a sand-filled minute glass instead. These can be found in many games and game stores in 2- or 3-minute versions.

I understand the desire to prepare students for the future timed tests of their lives, especially state standardized tests, the SAT, and the ACT. (By the way, a number of states have eliminated the time component of their state assessments. Can it be long before test constructors of every state understand the disadvantage of a timed test to visual-spatial learners?) But, if you're still using Mad Minutes in the classroom, I would like to invite you to go back to Chapter 9 for tips on teaching math facts in a more VSL-friendly way and to drop Mad Minutes altogether. Help your students to speed up the translation time from their images to words and numbers, not just the speedy recitation of facts.

Within the classroom, give your students, especially your visual-spatial learners, more time to consider a possible answer before calling on anyone. Extending your wait-time can increase the length and quality of your students' responses, allow greater participation (especially for your picture thinkers), and give all students time to incorporate more evidence in their answers.

chapter 14

Creating a Visual-Spatial Classroom

I hope that the real-life stories of visual-spatial kids who've found that these differentiation strategies helped them succeed in the classroom convince you to try them with your own students. Some of the tips, like using fantasy or incorporating metaphors, may take more preparation time than others. Some of the recommendations, such as offering alternative assignments to traditional book reports and research papers, may mean more work for you in the evaluation and assessment process, but most will add fun and entertainment to your day and lessons. All will make the learning more meaningful and permanent for each and every student you teach. In addition, a simple rubric of expectations serves as a useful measurement tool in evaluating a wide variety of assignments. Moving away from traditional left-hemispheric classrooms likely will be more meaningful for all of your students—visual-spatial and auditory-sequential—because those with strong right-hemispheric abilities will be allowed to call upon and use those strengths and those with strong left-hemispheric skills will be required to use their new knowledge in interesting and meaningful ways. Hardiman (2003) pointed out that when educators move away from traditional word-only assignments, more significant learning occurs:

> . . . as we have learned from the cognitive sciences, true learning occurs best when teachers require students not merely to acquire knowledge but to use it actively and meaningfully in real-world contexts. Such activities, which target both left-hemispheric language processing and right-hemispheric visual-spatial processing, motivate and stimulate students and promote creative thinking by encouraging the integration of the arts, technology, music, movement, dance, dramatizations, experiments, and inventions. (p. 71)

One campaign I would encourage every teacher to champion is to bring back the fine arts. In schools across the U.S., where budgets have been cut and programs have been sacrificed, it's been the arts—dance, drama, fine art, music—that have suffered. Here's an interesting point from David Sousa's *How the Brain Learns* (2006):

> We have never discovered a culture on this planet, past or present, that doesn't have art. Yet there have been a number of cultures—even today—that don't have reading and writing. Why is that? One likely explanation is that the activities represented by the arts—dance, music, drama, and visual arts—are basic to the human experience and necessary for survival. If they weren't, why would they have been part of every civilization from the Cro-Magnon cave dwellers to the urban citizens of the 21st century? (p. 213)

The Sights, Sounds, and Smells of Your Visual-Spatial Classroom

There is ample research to support that the actual environment a student is learning within—sights, sounds, and smells—plays a critical role in the comfort, attention level, and, ultimately, success of that student. Researchers (Hardiman, 2003; Jensen, 2005) found that students who attended an ideal class, where the lighting, acoustics, and design had been carefully orchestrated, performed significantly better in reading, listening, language, and math. They even demonstrated better discipline, greater attendance, and overall better health than students in less-optimal classrooms (Hardiman, 2003, p. 40). Did you know, for example, that the brain is extremely sensitive to temperature? "Reading comprehension declines when room temperature rises above 74 degrees Fahrenheit and math skills decline when it rises above 77 degrees Fahrenheit" (Jensen, 2005, p. 84). The ideal room temperature for optimal concentration and performance is 70 degrees Fahrenheit.

Taking in more than 36,000 images in an hour, our eyes and brain are on a never-ending quest for something new in their environment. Keeping your walls and boards stagnant has been directly linked to students drifting off-task and seeking stimulation through movement and other distractive behavior. So, change your room frequently. Subtle changes, particularly using materials related to the current learning, are best and work to satisfy the brain's quest for novelty. Be careful not to unintentionally create a visually distracting room, though. Careful use of the walls and ceiling is generally advisable, but suspending student projects too low, or from wall to wall, can interfere with their vision and space. And, while the official jury may still be in deliberation about wall color impacting student performance, researchers are leaning toward the following recommendations:

- use a warm yellow on the three walls that students face,

- use light blue on the rear wall—the wall the teacher faces,

- use contrasting cool colors as accents around the front of the room,

- use warmer colors (red and yellow) to stimulate students and cooler colors (light blue) to calm overactive students, and

- use a warm golden-gray on carpets. (Jensen, 2005, p. 90)

Like the hero in the movie *Joe Versus The Volcano*, too much fluorescent lighting can have a negative effect on the students in your classroom. Proper lighting, or the lack thereof, affects students' vision, comfort level, mood, and overall performance in school. As you might suspect, natural lighting is the best source.

In a study that examined the effects of natural light on the achievement of over 21,000 students in three school districts, researchers found that students in classrooms with the most natural lighting had from 7% to 18% higher test scores than those in classrooms with the least amount of natural lighting. (Hardiman, 2003, p. 42)

Try to eliminate glare, when possible, use warm yellows to paint walls or decorate with (to simulate natural light), and use a whiteboard instead of an overhead projector when teaching material that is important to see.

A lot of parents ask me about the background sound that their child claims to need in order to do homework—often this is music coming from an iPod. I side with the students on this one. I believe that a lot of kids have to have that background music playing in order to give their attention fully to the homework at hand. It's almost as though the music distracts the right hemisphere of the brain, giving it something to attend to, while the left hemisphere attends to the task at hand. As long as quality homework is the output, I have no objection to music during homework. In fact, I encourage it! If however, the music is a distraction for the whole brain, it has to go. Sounds in a classroom can be equally helpful or hurtful. There are reports of classical music improving students' performance in math, for example (Sousa, 2006). But, the use of music should be limited to times when students are working quietly and independently, not when the music has the potential to raise the volume of voices or when concentration is required. Noise, even music, can "interfere with the brain's ability to process auditory information and can interrupt cognitive processes" (Hardiman, 2003, p. 41).

What about the smells in your classroom? That can be as equally an important consideration as other environmental factors. Keeping in mind that many students, particularly the gifted, are very sensitive to perfumes and other scents, there are a number of studies that directly link the effects of peppermint, specifically, to improved mental performance. The ingredient reduced perceived physical workload, temporal workload, effort, and frustration among students. "The presence of peppermint was also found to improve mental ability with subjects making fewer errors and becoming more attentive" ("The Benefits of Peppermint Aroma," n.d., ¶ 6). Of course, I'm not suggesting you start handing out hard candy to your students—that would likely result in a whole host of justifiable complaints and concerns. But, just smelling the scent from an oil lamp, for instance, can have the same effect:

> In a study designed to determine the effects of pleasant scents on student behavior, Amie Gabriel (1999) dispensed one milliliter of scented oil into a metal oil-burning ring, which was placed on a 60-watt bulb 30 minutes prior to students' entry to the classroom. . . . She found a 54% reduction of off-task behaviors . . . (Hardiman, 2003, p. 42)

Getting Started

If you're ready to start creating a visual-spatial classroom right away, I applaud you! You will be immensely satisfied with the results. You will learn along the way what works and what doesn't, and you probably will come up with many of your own classroom strategies. If you feel you can't begin incorporating visual-spatial-friendly strategies for the whole class right away, try some of these ideas with one student who is failing. See what happens.

As you embark on reinventing your classroom, differentiating for the visual-spatial learners, and making it a more successful environment for all of your students, here are some simple guidelines to ask yourself:

1. Am I presenting the material visually?

2. Are there additional maps, diagrams, charts, photos, hands-on activities, or other materials I should incorporate?

3. Am I giving students enough time?

4. Are there opportunities for students to demonstrate mastery in visual-spatial-friendly ways?

5. Am I successfully differentiating by honoring each student for his or her preferred learning style?

If you find that you are having difficulty adding some of the suggested strategies to your classroom, the following list may help you come up with just the technique you need:

- overhead projector—what can you present on a transparency?

- computer—how can your students use classroom computers, the Internet, and computers at home to reinforce this lesson?

- diagrams, charts, graphs, movies, posters—how else can I present this material?

- maps, globes, atlases—how else can I show where the information is located?

- timelines, hands-on activities, field trips—how else can I show the when or who of the information?

- colored pens, folders, Post-it® Notes, index cards—how else can I help students get organized?

- manipulatives, games, demonstrations, experiments, models—how else can I show students the major points?

- dramatizations, role-playing, fantasy—how else can I engage students?

- metaphors, Venn diagrams—how I else can I help students see connections?

- dioramas, storyboards, puppet shows—how else can students show mastery?

- fidgets, doodling, walkabouts—how else can I accommodate kinesthetic needs?

I'd also like to encourage you to incorporate student portfolios in your class. These should be folders the students design, and the students should determine what is placed within the portfolio. It should be a reflection of their best work—not necessarily what they received the highest grade on, but the work of which they are the most proud. It could be something such as a spelling test they took after they tried a new, visual-spatial technique, or a report they wrote by starting with a web. At the end of this chapter, I've included a log for your students to record their work, why they selected it to be included in the portfolio, and the date. Encourage parents to come in and review their student's portfolio on occasion or use the portfolio during conferences.

These visual-spatial students of yours always will be picture-thinkers. They need to be motivated to use their talents and gifts, long after they've left your class. Encourage them to consider careers including higher level mathematics, science, invention, architecture, surgery, cartooning, aeronautics, and cartography. All of these careers require the ability to think in multiple dimensions and from varied perspectives.

Illustrated by Buck Jones. Copyright © held by Linda K. Silverman. From Silverman, L. K. (2002). *Upside-Down Brilliance: The Visual-Spatial Learner* (p. 332). Denver, CO: DeLeon Publishing. May not be reproduced without permission. Used with permission.

School probably will be the only time visual-spatial students feel they are not as bright or capable as their auditory-sequential friends. Beyond this time, in college and in the careers they choose, these children will begin to understand that the strengths of their right hemispheres are truly a gift. In creating a visual-spatial classroom, you can help them understand their gifts earlier and enjoy success in so many areas beyond the Three R's of 'ritin', readin' and 'rithmetic. Be their cheerleader, their mentor, and the adult in their lives, other than their parents, that truly cares about them. The strong emotional bond many visual-spatial students feel about the one teacher that truly understood them lasts their entire lifetime.

Be that teacher.

Portfolio Log

Use this log for students to record the work they select as their best examples. Invite parents to visit your classroom and review the log.

Example of My Work and Why I Chose It   **Date Entered**

_____   _____

_____

_____

_____   _____

_____

_____

_____   _____

_____

_____   _____

_____

_____   _____

_____

_____

Note. From *The Visual-Spatial Classroom: Differentiation Strategies That Engage Every Learner* (p. 137), by A. S. Golon, 2006, Denver, CO: Visual-Spatial Resource. Copyright © 2006 by Alexandra Shires Golon. Reprinted with permission.

References

The benefits of peppermint aroma. (n.d.). Retrieved January 24, 2008, from http://www.cosmeticsdesign.com/news/ng.asp?id=51092-the-benefits-of

Clare, J. D. (2004). *Differentiation.* Retrieved October 5, 2007, from http://www.greenfield.durham.sch.uk/differentiation.htm

DeVries, M., & Golon, A. S. (in press). Making education relevant for gifted Native Americans: Teaching to their learning style. In J. Castellano (Ed.), *A kaleidoscope of special populations in gifted education.* Waco, TX: Prufrock Press.

Golon, A. S. (2005). *If you could see the way I think: A handbook for visual-spatial kids.* Denver, CO: Visual-Spatial Resource.

Golon, A. S. (2006). *The visual-spatial classroom: Differentiation strategies that engage every learner.* Denver, CO: Visual-Spatial Resource.

Gurian, M. (2001). *Boys and girls learn differently! A guide for teachers and parents.* San Francisco: Wiley Company.

Hadamard, J. (1949). *The psychology of invention in the mathematical field.* Princeton, NJ: Princeton University Press.

Hall, T. (2002). *Differentiated instruction.* Wakefield, MA: National Center on Accessing the General Curriculum. Retrieved January 3, 2008, from http://www.cast.org/publications/ncac/ncac_diffinstruc.html

Hardiman, M. M. (2003). *Connecting brain research with effective teaching: The brain-targeted teaching model.* New York: Rowman & Littlefield Education.

Jensen, E. (2005) *Teaching with the brain in mind* (2nd ed.) Alexandria, VA: Association for Supervision and Curriculum Development.

Levine, M. (2002). *A mind at a time.* New York: Simon & Schuster.

Maxwell, E. (2003). Reading help for struggling gifted visual-spatial learners: Wholes and patterns. *Gifted Education Communicator, 34*(1), 23–24.

Ornstein, R. (1997). *The right mind: Making sense of the hemispheres.* New York: Harcourt Brace.

Pink, D. H. (2005). *A whole new mind: Moving from the information age to the conceptual age.* New York: Riverhead Books.

Ripley, A. (2005, March 7). Who says a woman can't be Einstein? *Time, 165,* 51–60.

Sax, L. (2005). *Why gender matters: What parents and teachers need to know about the emerging science of sex differences.* New York: Doubleday.

Silverman, L. K. (2002). *Upside-down brilliance: The visual-spatial learner.* Denver, CO: DeLeon Publishing.

Silverman, I., & Eals, M. (1992). Sex differences in spatial abilities: Evolutionary theory and data. In J. H. Barkow, L. Cosmides, & J. Tooby (Eds.), *The adapted mind* (pp. 533–549). New York: Oxford University Press.

Sousa, D. A. (2006). *How the brain learns* (3rd ed.). Thousand Oaks, CA: Corwin Press.

Springer, S. P., & Deutsch, G. (2001). *Left brain, right brain: Perspectives from cognitive neuroscience.* New York: W. H. Freeman.

Typing injuries frequently asked questions: Kids. (2007). Retrieved March 3, 2007, from http://www.tifaq.com/kids.html

Wallace, K. (2005, December). America's brain drain crisis: Why our best scientists are disappearing, and what's really at stake. *Reader's Digest.* Retrieved January 11, 2008, from http://www.rd.com/content/america-s-brain-drain-crisis

West, T. G. (2004). *Thinking like Einstein: Returning to our visual roots with the emerging revolution in computer information visualization.* New York: Prometheus.

Williams, L. V. (1983). *Teaching for the two-sided mind: A guide to right brain/left brain education.* New York: Simon & Schuster.

Wolfe, P. (2001). *Brain matters: Translating research into classroom practice.* Alexandria, VA: Association for Supervision and Curriculum Development.

About the Author

Alexandra "Allie" Golon is a Master Teacher at Rocky Mountain School for the Gifted & Creative in Boulder, CO. As a teacher and parent of gifted visual-spatial learners, Allie brings a wealth of experience to her books, *Raising Topsy-Turvy Kids: Successfully Parenting Your Visual-Spatial Child* and *If You Could See the Way I Think: A Handbook for Visual-Spatial Kids*. She has been invited to present on teaching and parenting visual-spatial learners at state, national, and international venues and has appeared on talk radio programs and in various print media. For more information, please visit Allie's Web site at http://www.Visual-Learners.com or write to her directly at Allie@Visual-Learners.com.